klaro!

a practical guide to
german grammar

klaro!

a practical guide to
german grammar

Susan Tebbutt

McGraw-Hill

Chicago New York San Francisco Lisbon London Madrid Mexico City
Milan New Delhi San Juan Seoul Singapore Sydney Toronto

Dedicated to
Clare and Graham

McGraw-Hill

A Division of The **McGraw·Hill** *Companies*

Library of Congress Cataloging-in-Publication Data
is available from the United States Library of Congress.

Cover design by Jennifer Locke

Originally published by Edward Arnold, a member of the Hodder Headline Group,
338 Euston Road, London NW1 3BH, UK
This edition first published by McGraw-Hill
A Division of The McGraw-Hill Companies
4255 West Touhy Avenue, Lincolnwood (Chicago), Illinois 60712-1975 U.S.A.
Copyright © 2001 by Susan Tebbutt
Printed in Malta by Gutenberg Press
International Standard Book Number: 0-07-138743-9
01 02 03 04   19 18 17 16 15 14 13 12 11 10 9 8 7 6 5 4 3 2 1

Contents

Acknowledgements

I would like to thank Peter Hohenhaus, Kirsten Guschal, Pamela Beimborn-Taylor, Anne White and my students for all their helpful comments.

How to use this book

You may consult this grammar practice book because:

- you know nothing about a particular grammar point;
- you know something but not everything about a grammar point;
- you want to revise what you once knew.

Structure of the book

Each chapter has a contents page and there is an index of grammatical topics at the end. References in the book may refer you to other sections. The grammar points are explained as simply as possible.

Terminology

As the terminology of grammar is complicated, a list of **grammatical definitions** has been included (see pages xi–xvi) before the grammar itself. This can either be read through first, or can be consulted when you meet a term that you don't understand.

Grammar sections

Each grammar section is numbered, and the rules of German grammar are explained in as brief and concise a way as possible.

Practice exercises

At the end of the sections explaining and illustrating grammatical points you will find sentences to help you practise using these rules. Some are gap-filling exercises and some involve translating from English into German. There are model answers to all the exercises at the end of the book.

Irregular verb tables

The verb is, of course, an extremely important area of grammar, and for this reason the main irregular verbs in German are given in the verb tables at the end of the book.

Tackling German grammar

German grammar is traditionally perceived as hard. Yet there are relatively few exceptions to the rules. It is important to break down the grammar into manageable sections and tackle one issue at a time. Each of the exercises in a particular section is loosely based on a theme (e.g. the workplace, the environment, travel, society, health). Vocabulary reinforcement and grammar practice are thus not seen as separate, but as complementary. The aim is to consolidate both the grammar and the vocabulary. Revision of grammar can be tied into a theme. Equally, revision of a theme can be tied in to grammar consolidation. The more you practise, the better you will get! Viel Spaß!

Grammatical definitions

English grammatical terms are written in bold type. A definition may include further grammatical terms. If you are uncertain of the meaning of a term, cross-reference it with its definition elsewhere in the table.

Term	German equivalent	Definition
Accusative	Akkusativ	One of four **cases** in German; mainly used for the **direct object** of a **transitive verb**
Adjective	Adjektiv	Word which makes a **noun** or **noun phrase** more precise
Adverb	Adverb	Word making a **verb, phrase** or **sentence** more precise
Affirmative	Affirmativ	An **affirmative** sentence makes a statement that is not **negative**
Agreement	Kongruenz	The **subject** of a **verb** determines the **verb**'s form; **number, gender** and **case** of a **noun** influence the form of any accompanying **adjective**
Apposition	Apposition	A **noun** is said to be in **apposition** with another **noun** when placed next to it to act as a definition
Article	Artikel	A word determining whether a **noun** is **definite** or **indefinite**
Auxiliary verb	Hilfsverb	The **verbs** *haben* and *sein* help to form the **compound tenses** and are known as **auxiliary** (helping) **verbs**

Term	German equivalent	Definition
Cardinal number	Kardinalzahl	One of series 1, 2, 3, etc. to infinity
Cases	Fälle	There are four **cases** in German, **Nominative**, **Accusative**, **Dative** and **Genitive**
Clause	Nebensatz/Klausel	Part of a **sentence** which contains a **subject** and a **verb**
Cognate	Kognate/verwandtes Wort	Word which has the same origin as another
Comparative	Komparativ	Form of the **adjective** or **adverb** expressing a comparison between one thing and another
Complement	Komplement	An element such as an **object** which follows a **verb**
Compound nouns	Komposita	**Nouns** made up of a **noun** and one or more other elements
Compound tense	zusammengesetztes Tempus	**Tense** consisting of **auxiliary verb** *haben* or *sein* and a **past participle**
Conditional	Konditional	**Tense** which tells what would happen if . . .
Conditional perfect	Konjunktiv II	**Tense** which tells what would have happened if . . .
Conjunction	Konjunktion	Word connecting sentences, clauses and words; there are **coordinating** and **subordinating conjunctions**
Coordinating conjunction	koordinierende Konjunktion	Links **clauses** of the same kind
Dative	Dativ	One of four **cases** in German
Definite article	bestimmter Artikel	A **noun** is **definite** if its identity is clear and/or known to the speaker; like 'the' in English
Demonstrative pronouns	Demonstrativpronomina	**Demonstrative pronouns** point out or refer to particular **nouns**

Term	German equivalent	Definition
Determiner	'Determiner'	Words used with a **noun** to link it to a particular context or situation, e.g. all, some
Direct object	direktes Objekt	**Noun** or **pronoun** which is the **direct object** of a **verb**
Direct speech	direkte Rede	Quotation of the actual words of a speaker
'False friend'	'falscher Freund'	Word which looks like an English word but has a different meaning
Feminine	Femininum	One of three **genders** in German
Finite verb	finites Verb	**Verb** which has indications of tense and agreement
Future	Futur	A **tense** which tells us what will happen in the **future**
Gender	Genus	There are three **genders** in German: **masculine**, **feminine** and **neuter**
Genitive	Genitiv	One of four **cases** in German
Imperative mood	Imperativ	The **imperative** is one of three **moods; mood** of the **verb** used for commands and invitations
Imperfect	Imperfekt	**Tense** which tells what was happening or used to happen
Impersonal verb	unpersönliches Verb	**Impersonal verbs** are introduced by es, and the es does not relate to anything
Indefinite article	unbestimmter Artikel	**Noun** said to be **indefinite** if its identity is unclear/unknown to the speaker; like 'a' in English
Indicative mood	Indikativ	One of three **moods**; the **mood** of the **verb** indicating fact
Indirect speech	indirekte Rede	Reported speech. e.g. She said that it was cold. He asked where it was.

Term	German equivalent	Definition
Infinitive	Infinitiv	Form of **verb** in dictionary; most **tenses** are formed from it.
Inseparable verb	untrennbares Verb	**Verb** with a **prefix** which remains attached to the root; **inseparable prefixes** are never stressed
Interjection	Interjektion	Word(s) thrown in to express emotion or attitude
Interrogative	Interrogativ	Question form
Intransitive verb	intransitives Verb	A **verb** which has no **object**
Inversion	Inversion	Reversing of order of two elements of a sentence
Main clause	Hauptsatz	**Clause** which makes complete sense on its own
Masculine	Maskulinum	One of three **genders** in German
Modal verb	Modalverb	**Verb** used to express possibility, obligation, etc.
Mood	Modus	The three **moods** are **imperative**, **indicative** and **subjunctive**
Negation	Negation	Process of making a **verb** or **noun**, etc. negative
Neuter	Neutrum	One of three **genders** in German
Nominative	Nominativ	One of four **cases** in German
Noun	Substantiv	A **noun** names a thing, person, place, quality or idea
Noun phrase	Nominalphrase	A group of words which together refer to something or someone; the **noun** is the most important element
Number	Numerus	All **nouns** and **pronouns** are either singular or plural
Object	Objekt	**Object** of a **verb**; can be **direct** or **indirect**
Ordinal number	Ordnungszahl	Part of series 1st, 2nd, 3rd, etc. to infinity

Term	German equivalent	Definition
Participle	Partizip	**Present participle** corresponds to English verb form ending in 'ing'; **past participle** is used to form past **compound tenses**, **passive** and **perfect infinitive**
Particle	Partikel	Word which expresses tone, intention or attitude e.g. *doch, ja, mal*
Passive	Passiv	Form of the **verb** in which the subject undergoes the action of the verb; formed with *werden* or *sein*
Past participle	Partizip Perfekt	**Past participle** is used to form past **compound tenses**, **passive** and **perfect infinitive**
Perfect	Perfekt	**Tense** formed with the **present tense** of the **auxiliary** verb *haben* or *sein* and **past participle**
Phrase	Phrase	Group of words lacking a **verb;** is smaller than a **clause** but still a complete unit of meaning
Pluperfect	Plusquamperfekt	Past tense which shows that one past action or event preceded another; like English 'had' + past participle
Possessive pronoun	Possessivpronomen	**Pronoun** showing ownership; refers to another **noun**
Prefix	Präfix	Element added before a **noun**, **adjective** or **verb** to make a different word
Preposition	Präposition	Word attached to a **noun** or certain other words to show position or relationship
Present participle	Partizip Präsens	Part of the **verb** which corresponds to the English **verb** form ending in 'ing'

Term	German equivalent	Definition
Pronoun	Pronomen	Stands for or replaces a **noun** or **noun phrase**
Reflexive verb	reflexives Verb	Type of **verb** which has a **reflexive pronoun** linked to it
Relative clause	Relativsatz	Modifies the sense of a **noun**, **noun phrase** or **pronoun**; **relative pronouns** send the **verb** to the end of the **clause**
Relative pronoun	Relativpronomen	Refers back to a **noun** or **noun phrase** used earlier; like 'who', 'which', 'whose', etc. in English
Separable verb	trennbares Verb	**Verb** with a **prefix** which may be separated from the root; **separable prefixes** are always stressed
Subject	Subjekt	**Noun**, **noun phrase** or **pronoun** in a **clause** or sentence which commits the action of a **verb**
Subjunctive mood	Konjunktiv	One of three **moods**
Subordinating conjunction	subordinierende Konjunktion	Links a main **clause** to a subordinate **clause**
Suffix	Suffix	Element added after a **noun**, **adjective** or **verb** to make a different word
Superlative	Superlativ	Form of the **adjective** or **adverb** which shows it is the largest, smallest, coldest, etc.
Transitive verb	transitives Verb	**Verb** which can have a direct object
Valency	Valenz	**Verbs** which are linked to a particular **preposition** or **case**
Verb	Verb	Word forming nucleus of a **sentence** or **clause** which refers to actions, processes, states, etc.

1

Basics

Contents

1.1 *German alphabet*

Letter	Approximate pronunciation
a	aa (as in English 'bar')
b	bay
c	tsay
d	day
e	eh (rhymes with English 'day')
f	eff
g	gay
h	haa
I	ee (rhymes with English 'see')
j	yot
k	kaa
l	ell
m	emm
n	enn
o	oh

Letter	Approximate pronunciation
p	pay
q	koo
r	err
s	ess
t	tay
u	ooh
v	fow (rhymes with English 'now')
w	vay
x	eeks
y	ipsilon
z	tsett
ß	ess-tsett
ä	e (as in English 'bed')
ö	i (as in English 'Sir')
ü	u (as in French 'tu'); lips rounded together as if about to whistle

Practise spelling your own name and the words in your address!

1.2 *Spelling, capitals and punctuation*

SPELLING

This volume conforms to the rules of the German *Rechtschreibreform* of 1 August 1998. Even after the Spelling Reform many publishers and newspapers still follow the old rules. The Reform does not apply in Switzerland, where *ss* is never written as *ß* but always as *ss*.

Rule	Old spelling	New spelling
ß after a short vowel is ss ß follows diphthongs (e.g. *weiß*) and long vowels (e.g. *Fuß, Spaß*)	ich muß ich weiß, daß es gut ist	ich muss ich weiß, dass es gut ist
Two infinitives used together are now separated	spazierengehen verlorengehen	spazieren gehen verloren gehen
Both the singular and plural forms of these two phrases are now separate	soviel; so viele wieviel; wie viele?	so viel; so viele wie viel?; wie viele?
Verbs and nouns are separated	radfahren	Rad fahren

Rule	Old spelling	New spelling
Times of day linked to *heute*, *gestern* or *morgen* are written with capital letters	gestern nachmittag heute abend	gestern Nachmittag heute Abend
Set phrases with adjectival nouns are now written with capitals	im ganzen im großen und ganzen im allgemeinen	im Ganzen im Großen und Ganzen im Allgemeinen
Three identical consonants together are now not reduced to two	Ballettänzer	Balletttänzer
Certain verbs are now more like their cognate nouns	numerieren plazieren	nummerieren platzieren
ck is no longer separated at all	lek-ker, Zuk-ker	lecker, Zucker
st is separated	We-ste	Wes-te

CAPITALS

One of the key differences between written English and written German is that in German all nouns are written with a capital. The following rules cover almost all cases except literary German, where rules may be broken for stylistic effect, e.g. in modern poetry.

Rule	Example
First word of a sentence is always written with a capital	Die Firma produziert Computer-Software.
All nouns are written with a capital letter	Berlin ist die Hauptstadt der BRD.
Other parts of speech used as nouns are written with a capital letter	Das Fotokopieren dauert sehr lange. Wir haben nichts Positives gehört.
Official titles and names of institutions and names referring to specific things are written with capital letters	Die Europäische Kommission hat ihren Sitz in Brüssel. Die Olympischen Spiele fanden 1936 in Berlin statt.
Adjectives of nationality are written with small letters	Sie arbeitete bei einer deutschen Firma.
The formal pronoun for 'you', *Sie*, is always written with a capital letter. The related adjective 'Ihr' also always has a capital letter.	Das ist warum Sie Ihre Dokumente mitnehmen müssen.
In correspondence *du* and *ihr* and the possessive adjectives are written with capital letters.	Liebe Michaela, wie geht es Dir? Was macht Ihr im Moment?

EXERCISE

A   Rewrite these sentences with capital letters in the correct places.

1   das reisen ist immer interessant.

2   Ich fliege am montag.

3   Wien ist die hauptstadt von österreich.

4   es ist spät.

5   gehen sie bitte zur passkontrolle.

6   der flughafen ist sehr groß.

7   es gibt einen flughafenbus.

8   der fahrer hat einen österreichischen Akzent.

PUNCTUATION

Commas are used more frequently than in English.

Rule	Example
Commas always precede subordinating conjunctions and relative pronouns	Sie arbeitet bis sechs, weil sie viel Arbeit hat. Sie ist die Frau, die immer bis spät arbeitet.
Commas separate off infinitive clauses with *um* + *zu* and an infinitive	Er wiederholt es, um es verständlicher zu machen.
Interjections are separated from the rest of the sentence by commas	Nein, das ist nicht möglich. Wir haben, offen gesagt, keine Probleme.
Two or more adjectives before a noun are separated by commas	Die neuen, progressiven Ideen sind sehr relevant.
Commas separate decimal points	4,5% (vier Komma fünf Prozent)
In German adverbs and adverbial phrases are not separated by commas from the rest of a clause	Heute sieht die Situation schlecht aus. Sie müssen trotzdem weiter investieren.
Full stops separate numbers from thousands, or a space may be left	5.000 or 5 000 25.000 or 25 000

1.3 *Cognates and 'false friends'*

COGNATE WORDS

Rule	German	English
b > v	sieben	seven
chs > x	nächste	next
d/t > th	danke	thanks
	tausend	thousand
j > y	ja	yes
k > c	Katze	cat
k > ch	Käse	cheese
mm > mb	Kamm	comb
pf > p	Pfeffer	pepper
pfl > pl	Pflaster	plaster
schw > sw	Schwindel	swindle
w > v	Wolga	Volga
z > t	zehn	ten
zw > tw	zwölf	twelve

EXERCISE

B Revise the guidelines on cognate words then give the English for the following.

1 Milch *milk*

2 Pfefferminz *peppermint*

3 Apfel *apple*

4 Pfannkuchen *pancake*

5 Karotte *carrot*

6 Joghurt *yoghurt*

7 Salz *salt*

8 Lamm *lamb*

9 Kaffee *coffee*

10 Wodka *vodka*

COGNATE ENDINGS

German ending	English ending	German	English
-anz	-ance/ancy	Eleganz Diskrepanz	elegance discrepancy
-bar	-ble	trinkbar	drinkable
-egie	-egy	Strategie	strategy
-ibel	-ible/able	flexibel	flexible
-ifizieren	-ify	modifizieren	modify
-ik	-ic/ics	Musik Aerobik	music aerobics
-isch	-ic/ical	realistisch biologisch	realistic biological
-isieren	-ise	kategorisieren	categorise
-ismus	-ism	Sozialismus	socialism
-ist	-ist	Pessimist	pessimist
-ität	-ity	Elektrizität	electricity
-lich	-ly	freundlich	friendly
-schaft	-ship	Freundschaft	friendship
-tionär	-tionary	reaktionär	reactionary
-ulieren	-ulate	regulieren	regulate
-voll	-ful	respektvoll	respectful

EXERCISE

C Revise the guidelines on cognate endings and give the English for the following words.

1 Intensität   *intensity*

2 politisch   *political*

3 Statistik   *statistic*

4 flexibel   *flexible*

5 harmonisieren   *harmonise*

6 Universität   *university*

7 Solidarität   *solidarity*

8 Optimismus   *optimism*

9 Taktik   *tactic*

10 revolutionär   *revolutionary*

'FALSE FRIENDS'

German	English
aktuell	topical
also	therefore
Art (f)	type, kind
bald	soon
Berliner (m)	person from Berlin; doughnut
Bett (nt)	bed
Branche (f)	sector of industry
Bürger (m)	citizen
Chef (m)	boss
Chips (pl)	crisps
Dom (m)	cathedral
Dose (f)	can, tin
elf	eleven
engagiert	committed, involved
eventuell	possibly
Fahrt (f)	journey
Gasthaus (nt)	inn, restaurant
Gift (nt)	poison
groß	large, tall
gut	good
Gymnasium (nt)	grammar school
Herd (m)	cooker
Hose (f)	trousers
Kanne (f)	teapot, coffeepot
Kost (f)	food, fare
Lager (nt)	camp
Land (nt)	country, federal state (e.g. Bavaria)
leer	empty
List (f)	trick, cunning
Lyrik (f)	poetry
Mappe (f)	document case
Marmelade (f)	jam

German	English
Menü (nt)	set meal
Messe (f)	trade fair; church mass
Mist (m)	dung
Mode (f)	fashion
necken	to tease
Not (f)	emergency (*Notausgang* (m) = emergency exit)
Note (f)	mark, grade
Pass (m)	passport
Pension (f)	guest-house
Personal (nt)	staff
Pickel (m)	spot, pimple
Plastik (f)	piece of sculpture
Prospekt (m)	brochure
Puff (m)	brothel
Puzzle (nt)	jigsaw
Rat (m)	advice, council
Rente (f)	pension
Ringer (m)	wrestler
Rock (m)	skirt
See (m)	lake (*See* (f) = sea)
Sekt (m)	sparkling wine
Sender (m)	radio station, transmitter
sensibel	sensitive
Slip (m)	pants, underpants
Smoking (m)	dinner jacket
sparen	to save
spenden	to donate
Spot (m)	commercial, ad
Sympathie (f)	affection
Tablett (nt)	tray
trampen	to hitchhike
turnen	to do gymnastics
wandern	to hike
wanken	to stagger

EXERCISE

D Revise the list of 'false friends' and translate the following sentences into English.

1 Das Restaurant lag direkt am See.

2 In der Ecke gab es eine Plastik.

3 Der Kellner hatte viele Pickel.

4 Die Kellnerin trug einen schwarzen Rock.

5 Der Gast trug einen Smoking.

6 Wieviel Geld hat die Firma für das Essen gespendet?
donate

7 Wir haben den neuen Chef gesehen.

8 Der Kellner trug die Gläser auf einem Tablett.

9 Zum Frühstück gab es Brötchen mit Marmelade und Butter.

10 An der Bar verkaufen sie Chips.

1.4 *Dictionary use, word formation, prefixes and suffixes*

Not all German words are in the dictionary, since it is possible to combine many elements to make new words. Compound nouns can be formed from two or more nouns, or from a noun and another element. If the compound noun is not listed you should look up the final element. The earlier parts define it.

COMPOUND NOUNS

Rule	Example	Meaning
Gender of a compound noun is that of its final part	der Fußball*platz* die Fußball*mannschaft* das Fußball*stadion*	the football ground the football team the football stadium
Two nouns can be linked by a hyphen (now very common)	die Computer-Software	computer software
Administrative regions where each part has equal status are linked by a hyphen	Nordrhein-Westfalen	North Rhine Westfalia
Two nouns may be linked	Politikstudent	politics student
Two or more nouns may be linked by an *s* or *es*	Arbeitsmöglichkeit Jahresende	opportunity for work end of the year
Compound nouns may translate into English as the xxx of xxx	Abteilungsleiter	head of department

SOME COMPOUND NOUNS HAVE SET MEANINGS

Compound noun	Meaning of the elements	Actual meaning
Bodensee (m)	floor + sea/lake	Lake Constance
Eishalle (f)	ice + hall	ice rink
Fußgängerzone (f)	foot + goer + zone	pedestrian precinct
Kaufhaus (nt)	purchase + house	department store
Kinderwagen (m)	children + car	pram
Mittelmeer (nt)	middle + sea	Mediterranean
Parkhaus (nt)	park + house	multi-storey carpark

EXERCISE

E What do the following mean? What gender are they?

1 Umweltpolitik *(die) environmental politics/policy*

2 Umweltministerium *(das) Ministry of the environment*

3 Umweltfrage *(die)*

4 Umweltminister *(der)*

5 Umweltstrategie

PREFIXES (* = Inseparable)

Prefix	General idea	Example	Meaning
ab-	away	abfahren	to depart, go away
an-	approaching	ankommen	to arrive
auf-	up	aufessen	to eat up
	on	aufsetzen	to put on (e.g. hat)
aus-	out	ausgehen	to go out
	completion	austrinken	to drink up
auseinander-	apart	auseinandergehen	to come apart
be-*	makes intransitive verbs transitive	beantworten	to answer
durch-	through	durchkommen	to get through
ein-	in; getting used to something	sich einleben	to settle in
ent-*	getting away	entkommen	to escape
entgegen-	towards	entgegenkommen	to come towards s-th/sb

Prefix	General idea	Example	Meaning
er-*	completion of an action	erschießen	to shoot dead
ge-	at beginning of most past participles	gespielt gegangen	played went
los-	setting off; going away	losgehen	to set off
miss-*	bad; wrong	missverstehen	to misunderstand
mit-	with	mitgehen	to accompany
nieder-	down; lower	niederlassen	to put down
über-	over; too much	überfahren	to run over
um-	turning round changing state	umsehen umsteigen	to look around to change (trains, etc.)
ver-*	mistake excess problem	sich verfahren versalzen verarmen	to go the wrong way to add too much salt to become poor
voll-	full; completion	volltanken	to fill up with petrol
vor-	forward in front	vorgehen vorspringen	to be fast (watches) to jump in front
weg-	away	wegbringen	to take away
wieder-	again	wiedersehen	to see again
zer-*	into pieces	zerbrechen	to smash into pieces
zurück-	back	zurückgeben	to give back

EXERCISE

F Revise the meanings of the prefixes and match the verbs and their meanings.

1	zurückspringen ⊂	**A**	to run out
2	durchfahren f	**B**	to go down
3	misshandeln i	**C**	to jump back
4	zerreißen g	**D**	to set off
5	auslaufen a	**E**	to fill up
6	niedergehen b	**F**	to drive through
7	losfahren d	**G**	to tear to pieces
8	vollfüllen e	**H**	to oversleep
9	auseinanderfallen j	**I**	to maltreat, abuse
10	verschlafen h	**J**	to fall apart

SUFFIXES

Suffixes can be added to the end of words. Nouns can be formed from verbs or adjectives by adding suffixes.

Suffix	Meaning	Example	Exceptions
-in	Feminine person	Touristin	Nikotin (nt)
-er	Inhabitant of a town	ein Heidelberger	
	Adjective describing	der Kölner Dom	
	something from a town		
	Formed from verbs;	der Spieler	
	someone doing that action	der Fahrer	
-chen and -lein (noun often adds umlaut)	Diminutive form of a noun	das Brötchen das Fräulein	
-bar (added to verb stem)	Corresponds to English -ible/-able	trinkbar essbar	
-mässig	According to	instinktmässig (English: instinctively)	
-erweise (added to adjective)	In a particular way	freundlicherweise (English: in a friendly way)	

EXERCISES

G   Revise the meanings of the suffixes and match the words and their meanings.

1   die Schauspielerin *b*   **A** normally

2   der Bonner *d*   **B** actress

3   normalerweise *a*   **C** painter

4   spielbar *e*   **D** man from Bonn

5   Maler *C*   **E** playable

H   Now give the German for each of the following.

1   woman artist Malerin

2   woman from Hamburg Hamburgerin

3   actor Schauspieler

4   in a nice way ~~schönweise~~ netterweise

5   readable ~~lesebar~~ lesbar

2

Cases

Contents

2.1 Use of Nominative case

2.2 Use of Accusative case

2.3 Use of Dative case

2.4 Use of Genitive case

There are four cases in German. They are Nominative, Accusative, Dative and Genitive. In all the tables in this volume they appear in this order. The Genitive is placed last because it is the least used in modern German.

The forms of the definite article are as follows. (See Chapter 5 for more on **Nouns** and Chapter 6 for more on **Articles**.)

Definite article: 'the'

	M	F	N	Pl
Nom.	der	die	das	die
Acc.	den	die	das	die
Dat.	dem	der	dem	den
Gen.	des	der	des	der

2.1 *Use of Nominative case*

Rule	Example
Nominative case is used for the subject of a verb.	*Der Mann* spielt Tennis.
The verb *sein* always takes the Nominative case.	Helmut Kohl war *der Bundeskanzler.*
The verb *bleiben* always takes the Nominative case	Er bleibt *der Manager.*

2.2 *Use of Accusative case*

Rule	Example	Exception
Accusative is used for the direct object of a verb.	Ich sehe *den Mann.* Wir sehen *die neuen Gebäude.*	Certain verbs take the Dative case in German. (See Chapter 10.)
es *gibt* + Accusative	Es gibt *einen Plan.*	
Accusative is used for time phrases when indicating length of time or a specific point in time	Wir waren *einen Monat* in Paris. *Nächsten Freitag* besuchen wir die Firma. *Jeden Donnerstag* gehen wir schwimmen.	Phrases with prepositions and Dative e.g. *am Donnerstag* *im November* Genitive phrases referring to regular events e.g. *abends* (every evening)
Used after prepositions + Accusative (See Chapter 9.)	Ich kaufte es für *den Manager.*	
Used after prepositions + Accusative when movement is involved (See Chapter 9.)	Wir gingen in *den Park.* Sie fahren *ans Meer* (= an *das* Meer).	
Used after certain verbs + prepositions + Accusative (See Chapter 10.)	Ich interessiere mich für *den Wagen.*	
Used after certain adjectives + Accusative (See Chapter 8.)	Ich bin *es* satt.	

EXERCISE

A   Revise the information on Nominative and Accusative and insert the correct form of the definite article in each sentence.

1   Wo ist _der_ Dom? (der)

2   Ich habe _den_ Weihnachtsmarkt besucht. (der)

3   Sie ist in _die_ Stadt gegangen. (die)

4   _Das_ Rathaus liegt in der Altstadt. (das)

5   Ich verbringe _den_ Vormittag in der Stadtmitte. (der)

6   Ohne _die_ Fußgängerzone wäre die Stadt nicht so umweltfreundlich. (die)

7   _Der_ Bahnhof ist ganz modern. (der)

8   Ich habe _den_ Stadtpark gesehen. (der)

9   Wir wandern durch _den_ Thüringer Wald. (der)

10   _Der_ Nationalpark ist fantastisch. (der)

2.3 Use of Dative case

Rule	Example
Used for the indirect object. Used for giving sth to sb or taking sth from sb.	Er gibt es *dem Freund*. Er nahm es *mir*.
Used after prepositions + Dative (See Chapter 9.)	Er ging mit *dem Abteilungsleiter*. Sie kam aus *dem Haus*.
Used after prepositions + Dative when no movement is involved. (See Chapter 9.)	Wir waren vor *dem Rathaus*.
Used after certain verbs + Dative (See Chapter 10.)	Er imponierte *mir*. Sie half *der Frau* im Supermarkt.
Used after verbs and prepositions + Dative (See Chapter 10.)	Sie telefoniert mit *dem Millionär*.
Used with certain adjectives + Dative (See Chapter 8.)	Der Marketing-Manager ist *mir* bekannt.

NB In the Dative Plural nouns add an *-n* if they do not already end in *-n*.

Noun and plural	Use of Dative Plural	Meaning
das Jahr, -e	Wir machen das seit 4 *Jahren*.	We have been doing that for 4 years.
der Tag, -e	Vor 5 *Tagen* hat es geschneit.	It snowed 5 days ago.
die Zeit, -en	Zu diesen *Zeiten* ist das Büro geschlossen.	The office is closed at these times.

2.4 Use of Genitive case

Rule	Example	Exception
Genitive is used to express possession, or the English 'of'	Der Bruder *meines Vaters* ist krank. Dies ist die Aufgabe des *Verkaufsleiters*.	*Von* is also often used to indicate possession. Er ist der Bruder *von meiner Chefin*.
First names may add an 's', similar to the English use of the apostrophe + s	Das ist *Marias* Computer.	When first name and surname are given, use *von* + Dative. Das ist der Computer *von* Christa Mayer. With titles like *Herr* or *Dr. von* + Dative is used. Das sind die Pläne *von Herrn Schmidt*. Das ist das Haus *von Dr. Dietze*.

Rule	Example	Exception
Used for indefinite time expressions	*eines Tages* one day	
Used for regular times or days when something happens	*morgens* every morning *vormittags* every morning *nachmittags* every afternoon *abends* every evening *sonntags* every Sunday *wochentags* on weekdays	
Used with prepositions + Genitive (See Chapter 9.)	Trotz *des schlechten Wetters* spielen sie Golf.	

NB In the singular most Masculine and Neuter nouns add *-s* or *-es* in the Genitive case.

Noun	Genitive Singular	Meaning
der Krieg, -e	Am Ende des *Kriegs* waren viele Leute obdachlos.	At the end of the war many people were homeless.
der Monat, -e	Am Anfang des *Monats* habe ich genug Geld.	At the start of the month I have enough money.
das Jahr, -e	Am Ende des *Jahres* werden wir feiern.	We will celebrate at the end of the year.

EXERCISES

B Revise the Genitive and Dative and insert the correct form of the definite article in each sentence.

1 Trotz _des_ Regens war es ein schöner Urlaub. (der)

2 Sie kamen aus _der_ Türkei. (die)

3 Sie arbeitet bei _der_ großen Reisefirma. (die)

4 Das ist die Zentrale _der_ Firma. (die)

5 Wegen _des_ Gewitters konnten wir nicht Wasserski fahren. (das)

6 Sie gab _den_ Touristen die Informationen. (die)

7 Das Museum imponierte _den_ Besuchern. (die)

8 Das Planetarium gehört _der_ Stadt. (die)

9 Das Fußballstadion war neben _dem_ Sportzentrum. (das)

10 Sie beschäftigten sich mit _der_ Stadtgeschichte. (die)

C   What case are the italicized words and why?

1   *Der Mann* arbeitet bei einer neuen Firma.   NOM

2   Wir haben *den Mann* gesehen.   AKK

3   Ich habe *dem Mann* die Informationen gegeben.   DAT

4   Es war die Aufgabe *des Mannes*, neue Strukturen einzuführen.   GEN

5   *Letztes Jahr* haben sie neue Systeme entwickelt.   ~~GEN~~ AKK

6   *Nächsten Monat* werden wir die Filiale in der Tschechischen Republik besuchen.   AKK

7   Sie organisierten das für *die ganze Firma*.   AKK

8   Er ist *der letzte Vertreter* der alten Organisation.   NOM
                           der

9   Es gibt *einen guten Flohmarkt*.   AKK

10   Er kommt aus *der Türkei*.   DAT

11   Sie machten es wegen *der Kontinuität*.   ~~DAT~~ GEN

12   Es hängt von *der wirtschaftlichen Situation* ab.   DAT
                               die

13   Sie erklären das *den Arbeitern*.   DAT

14   Wir fahren *nächsten Dienstag*.   AKK

15   *Vormittags* gibt es immer eine Besprechung.   GEN

16   Sie versteht die Analyse *der Situation* sehr gut.   ~~DAT~~ GEN
                            die

17   Das ist *das Problem* der neuen Mitarbeiter.   NOM

18   Wir sprechen über *die Strategie*.   AKK

19   Sie besprechen *die neue Lage*.   AKK

20   *Eines Tages* wird es leichter sein.   GEN

trotz = in spite of

3 Word order and conjunctions

Contents

3.1 Verb second idea

In German the **verb** is normally the **second idea**. In the following examples the main verb is italicized. The item preceding the verb can be:

The subject	Wir *arbeiten* bei Siemens.
	Der Manager *wohnt* in Hamburg.
A question word e.g. *was, warum*	Was *machen* Sie?
A word or phrase	Nächstes Jahr *exportieren* wir nach Japan.
A whole clause	Weil das Wetter so schön ist, *spielen* wir Tennis.

NB Elements of the sentence, including the direct or indirect object, can be emphasized by placing them first. The **verb** is still the **second idea**.

Rule	Example
Direct object first for emphasis	Den Mann *hatte* ich gestern gesehen.
Indirect object first for emphasis	Ihm *haben* wir geholfen.

3.2 *Interjections*

If there is an interjection at the beginning of the sentence it is followed by a comma, then the subject. The most common interjections are:

Interjection	Meaning	Example
ach	oh	Ach, es ist zu schwer.
das heißt	that is to say	Das heißt, es gibt viele Probleme.
ehrlich gesagt	to be honest	Ehrlich gesagt, ich finde es problematisch.
im Gegenteil	on the contrary	Im Gegenteil, ich kann das gut verstehen.
ja	yes	Ja, es ist OK.
kurz	in short	Kurz, es wird zu problematisch sein.
mit anderen Worten	in other words	Mit anderen Worten, ich finde es unmöglich.
nein	no	Nein, wir können das nicht akzeptieren.
offen gesagt	to be frank	Offen gesagt, das kommt nicht in Frage.
übrigens	incidentally	Übrigens, es kostet viel mehr als erwartet.
unter uns	between ourselves	Unter uns, die Situation sieht schlecht aus.
wie gesagt	as I said	Wie gesagt, wir müssen mehr exportieren.
zum Beispiel	for example	Zum Beispiel, sie arbeiten mit französischen Firmen.

EXERCISES

A Underline the main verb in each sentence.

1 Die Galerie besitzt viele Bilder aus dem 19. Jahrhundert.

2 In dieser Galerie sehen wir viele Lithographien.

3 Offen gesagt, die Installationen sind nicht besonders interessant.

4 Weil die Bilder so schön sind, müssen sie hinter Glas sein.

5 Wie finden Sie dieses Stillleben?

6 Im Dritten Reich wurden viele Bilder verboten.

7 Übrigens, das Museum ist donnerstags bis 20.00 geöffnet.

8 Letztes Jahr gab es eine fantastische Kirchner-Ausstellung.

B   Give the German for the following sentences.

1   In short, the museum is very interesting. *Kurz, das Museum ist sehr interessant.*

2   To be frank, I have not much time. *Offen gesagt, ich habe ~~keine~~ nicht viel Zeit.*

3   As I said, I have to visit the exhibition. *Wie gesagt, ich ~~habe~~ muss die Austellung besuchen.*

4   In other words, it is not easy. *Mit anderen Worten, es ist nicht leicht.*

5   To be honest, it is impossible. *Erlich gesagt, es'es ist unmöglich.*

3.3 Verb first idea

There are only three reasons why the verb is first in a sentence.

Rule	Example	Meaning
Questions (except those starting with a question word like *wer*, *wo* or *wann*)	*Gehen Sie in die Stadt?*	Are you going to town?
Commands	*Gehen Sie in die Stadt!*	Go to town!
Conditional clauses without the word *wenn* (See Chapter 10.)	*Gehen Sie in die Stadt, so werden Sie viele Touristen sehen.*	If you go into town you will see a lot of tourists.

VERB FIRST: QUESTIONS

Questions are formed by inverting the subject and object. It is easy to make a statement into a question.

e.g. *Statement*: Es ist kalt. *Question*: Ist es kalt?

EXERCISE

C   Now make the following statements into questions.

1   Es ist sonnig in Rostock.   *Ist es sonnig in Rostock?*

2   Es hat viel geregnet.   *Hat es viel geregnet?*

3   Es kann später windiger werden.   *Kann es später windiger werden?*

4   Es gibt viele Wolken.   *Gibt es viele Wolken?*

5   Trotz des schlechten Wetters war es ein Erfolg.   *War es*

VERB FIRST: COMMANDS

Commands begin with the verb. (See Chapter 10.)

Person	Rule	Example
du	Stem of verb (See Chapter 10 for exceptions.)	*Geh* in die Stadt! Go into town!
wir	Infinitive + *wir*	*Gehen wir* in die Stadt! Let's go into town!
Sie	Infinitive + *Sie*	*Geben Sie* mir die Karten! Give me the tickets!
ihr	Stem of verb + t	*Bringt* mir die Bilder! Bring me the pictures!

EXERCISE

D Translate the following commands into German, using the form given.

nehmen   1   Take the second street left. (ihr) Nehmt die zweite Strasse.links

zeigen   2   Show me the town plan. (Sie) Zeigen Sie mir den Stadtplan.

warten   3   Wait in front of the town hall. (du) Warte von dem Rathaus

parken   4   Let's park behind the supermarket. (wir) Parken wir hinter dem SM.

bringen   5   Bring me the tickets. (Sie) Bringen Sie mir die Tickets, Karten.

VERB FIRST: CONDITIONAL CLAUSES WITHOUT 'WENN'

If the word *wenn* is omitted from a conditional sentence, the verb comes first and the subject second.

Conditional sentence with 'wenn'	Conditional clause without 'wenn'	Meaning
Wenn es schön ist, gehe ich schwimmen.	*Ist* es schön, gehe ich schwimmen.	If it's nice I go for a swim.
Wenn ich es gemacht hätte, wäre es besser gewesen.	*Hätte* ich es gemacht, wäre es besser gewesen.	If I had done it, it would have been better.

EXERCISE

E Rewrite the following sentences without *wenn*.

1 Wenn es kalt ist, bleiben wir zu Hause. *Ist es kalt, bleiben wir zu H.*

2 Wenn ich Zeit habe, lese ich die Zeitung. *Habe ich Zeit, lese ich die Zeitung*

3 Wenn Sie in die Disko gehen, rufen Sie uns an. *Gehen Sie in die Disko, rufen Sie uns an.*

4 Wenn er Geld hat, kauft er CDs. *Hat er Geld, kauft er CDs.*

5 Wenn sie Zeit haben, hören sie Volksmusik. *Haben sie Zeit, hören sie V.*

3.4 *Coordinating conjunctions*

After coordinating conjunctions the **subject** is **followed by the verb**. If the subject is the same in both clauses it is possible to omit the subject in the second clause.

Conjunction	Meaning	Example
aber	but	Ich gehe in die Stadt, aber er *bleibt* zu Hause.
denn	as, because	Sie protestieren, denn die Benzinpreise *sind* zu hoch.
entweder . . . oder	either . . . or	Entweder sie *fahren* mit der Bahn, oder sie *nehmen* ein Taxi.
oder	or	Ich schicke es morgen, oder mein Chef *schickt* ein Fax.
sondern	but (after a negative)	Er exportiert nicht, sondern *konzentriert* sich auf den Inlandsmarkt.
und	and	Sie expandieren in Deutschland, und *haben* neue Pläne für die USA.

EXERCISE

F Link the two sentences with the coordinating conjunctions given.

1 Sie ist die Leiterin. Sie ist sehr streng. (und)
Sie ist die Leiterin, und (sie) ist sehr streng.

2 Die Region hat große Probleme mit Arbeitslosigkeit. Es ist besonders schlimm auf dem Lande. (aber)
, aber es ist ...

3 Er übersetzt Texte aus dem Deutschen ins Englische. Er hilft seinen Kollegen. (oder)
, oder er hilft ...

4 Sie machten ein Praktikum in Deutschland. Sie lernen da viel Deutsch. (denn)
, denn sie lernen ...

5 Meine Kollegen arbeiten bis 6 Uhr. Ich arbeite bis 4. (aber)
, aber ich arbeite ...

3.5 *Subordinating conjunctions: word order rules*

Rule	Example	Meaning
Subordinating conjunctions are followed by subject + rest of clause + verb at end of clause.	Als ich in Aachen *arbeitete* . . .	When I worked in Aachen . . .
If there is a finite verb + infinitive, the finite verb goes at end of clause.	Als ich in Aachen arbeiten *musste*, war es schwer.	When I had to work in Aachen it was difficult.
With a compound tense of a modal and an infinitive (i.e three verbs together), the finite verb comes first of the three verb forms	Weil er es *hatte* machen können, . . . Weil ich es *habe* hören können, . . .	Because he had been able to do it . . . Because I have been able to hear it . . .

SUBORDINATING CONJUNCTIONS

Conjunction	Meaning	Example
als	when	Als ich es sah, wollte ich es kaufen.
bevor	before	Bevor wir nach Spanien fuhren, mussten wir Geld umtauschen.
bis	until	Bis ich 18 war, bin ich nicht viel gereist.
da	as	Da es so kalt ist, wollen wir zu Hause bleiben.
damit	in order that	Damit ich mehr von der Region sehe, habe ich ein Auto gemietet.
dass	that	Ich weiß, dass es eine sehr schöne Stadt ist.
nachdem	after	Nachdem wir das Museum besucht hatten, wollten wir mehr über die Expressionisten lernen.
ob	whether	Sie wissen nicht, ob das Museum geöffnet ist.
obwohl, obgleich, obschon (obschon is the least common of the three)	although	Obwohl die Galerie klein ist, finde ich sie sehr interessant.
seitdem	since (used in time phrases)	Seitdem ich in der Stadtmitte arbeite, fahre ich immer mit dem Bus.
sobald	as soon as	Sobald es möglich ist, werde ich mein Auto verkaufen.

Conjunction	Meaning	Example
solange	as long as	Solange wir nichts hören, können wir nichts tun.
während	whereas, while	Ich mag Jazz, während er Popmusik mag.
weil	because	Es ist teuer, weil die Benzinkosten hoch sind.
wenn	if, whenever	Wenn ich Zeit habe, gehe ich ins Kino.
wie	as	Wie Sie wissen, habe ich einen Onkel in Bonn.
	how (with reported questions in indirect speech)	Ich verstehe, wie Sie das machen.
zumal	especially as	Es ist billig, zumal ich bei meinem Onkel wohnen kann.

erfolgreich = successful
verantwortlich = responsible

EXERCISE

G Revise the rules about subordinating conjunctions. Link the two sentences with the conjunction given.

1 Der Chef diktiert die Briefe. Die Sekretärin tippt sie. (während)
   , während die Sekretärin sie tippt.

2 Die Firma expandiert. Das Produkt ist sehr erfolgreich. (weil)
   , weil das Produkt sehr erfolgreich ist.

3 Sie arbeiten den ganzen Nachmittag. Sie sind sehr müde. (obwohl)
   , obwohl sie sehr müde sind.

4 Die Filiale hat sehr viel Arbeit. Sie ist für die ganze Region verantwortlich. (zumal)
   , zumal sie für die ganze Region verantwortlich ist.

5 Sie machten viele Überstunden. Ich war in der Abteilung. (als)
   , als ich in der Abteilung war.

6 Die Firma hatte ihren Hauptsitz in Bochum. Sie ist nach Stuttgart gezogen. (bevor)
   , bevor sie nach Stuttgart gezogen ist.

7 Sie haben die Firma umstrukturiert. Sie machen mehr Profit. (damit)
   , damit sie mehr Profit machen.

8 Sie waren viel erfolgreicher. Die Firma hatte diversifiziert. (nachdem)
   , nachdem die Firma diversifiziert hatte.

9 Die Produkte sind sehr beliebt. Sie sind sehr teuer. (obwohl)
   , obwohl sie sehr teuer sind.

10 Mehr Leute haben von der Firma gehört. Sie machen mehr Fernsehspots. (seitdem)
   , seitdem sie mehr Fernsehspots machen.

3.6 *Omission of* dass

It is possible to omit the subordinating conjunction *dass*. This is usually done to make a sentence less clumsy, especially if there are quite a number of verbs in a sentence. If *dass* is omitted, the subject comes first in the clause, followed immediately by the finite verb.

Subordinate clause with *dass*	Omission of *dass*	Meaning
Wir haben gehört, dass es sehr schwer ist.	Wir haben gehört, es ist sehr schwer.	We have heard that it is very hard.
Ich muss sagen, dass ich ins Konzert gehen wollte.	Ich muss sagen, ich wollte ins Konzert gehen.	I must say that I wanted to go to the concert.
Sie sagte, dass sie hoffte, in die USA zu fahren.	Sie sagte, sie hoffte, in die USA zu fahren.	She said she was hoping to go to the USA.

EXERCISE

H   Rewrite the following sentences without *dass*.

1   Ich habe gehört, dass Schindler vielen Menschen geholfen hat.

2   Man sagt, dass jemand einen Koffer mit Schindlers Liste gefunden hat.

3   Die Zeitung berichtet, dass der Koffer einer Frau in Hildesheim gehörte.

4   Sie sagen, dass Schindler jetzt krank ist.

5   Viele Leute sagen, dass der Film *Schindlers Liste* interessant ist.

6   Andere denken, dass der Film problematisch ist.

7   Einige behaupten, dass er zu melodramatisch ist.

8   Kritiker sagen, dass der Film alles zu sentimental darstellt.

3.7 *Separable prefixes and past participles*

Certain elements go to the end of the clause.

Rule	Example
Separable prefix	Ich stehe um 9 Uhr *auf*.
Separable prefix joins verb in relative clauses	Das ist die Frau, die mit ihr *zusammenarbeitet*.
The past participle	Er hat das Buch gestern *gelesen*.
Separable prefix joined to past participle	Sie ist um 10 *zurückgekommen*.

EXERCISE

I   Give the German for the following sentences.

1   He gets up at 8. (aufstehen)   *Er steht um 8 Uhr auf.*

2   He goes back to the sports centre. (zurückgehen)   *Er geht zum Sportzentrum zurück.*

3   Our friends came back at 4. (zurückkommen)   *Unsere Freude zurückgekommen un 4 Uhr.*

4   That is the woman who arrived yesterday. (ankommen)   *Das ist die Frau, die gestern angekommen.*

5   They spent DM 200 in the sports shop. (ausgeben)   *Sie haben DM 200 im Sportgeschaft ausgegeben.*

3.8 *Word order in relative clauses*

Relative pronouns send the **main verb to the end of the clause**. Here is a reminder of the forms of the **Relative Pronoun**. (See Chapter 7 for more on Pronouns.)

	M	F	N	Pl
Nom.	der	die	das	die
Acc.	den	die	das	die
Dat.	dem	der	dem	denen
Gen.	dessen	deren	dessen	deren

EXERCISE

J   Revise rules on Relative Pronouns and word order and then rewrite the sentences with the last four words in each sentence in the right order.

1   Sie ist die Frau, trinkt die viel Bier.   *, die viel Bier trinkt.*

2   Das ist der Koch, gute der macht Salate.   *, der gute Salate macht.*

3   Das ist die Pizzeria, der arbeitete ich in.   *, in der ich arbeitete.*

4   Wo ist die Kellnerin, uns bediente alle die?   *, die uns alle bediente.*

5   Ich dachte an das Wirtshaus, gute Fischgerichte das macht.   *, das gute F. macht.*

3.9 *Positioning infinitives and modal verbs*

Infinitives used after modal verbs (*dürfen, können, mögen, müssen, sollen, wollen*), and *werden* and *lassen* **go to the end of the clause**. In subordinate clauses the finite verb is at the end.

Rule	Example	Meaning
Infinitive goes at end of clause after a modal verb	Darf ich Ihnen ein Stück Torte *anbieten*?	May I offer you a piece of cake?
Infinitive goes at end after *um + zu*	Ich ging ins Restaurant, um Pizza zu *essen*.	I went into the restaurant to eat pizza.
Infinitive goes at end of clause after *werden*	Wir werden alle zusammen *essen*.	We will all eat together.
Infinitive goes at end of clause after *lassen*	Ich lasse die Nachspeise jetzt *servieren*.	I will have the dessert served now. (NB Present Tense. See Chapter 10.)
Finite verb comes after the infinitive in subordinate clauses	Alles ist OK, weil sie das Essen jetzt *kaufen* kann	Everything is OK because she can buy the food now.
When there are three verb forms in a subordinate clause, the finite verb comes first of the three forms	Jetzt können sie das Restaurant empfehlen, weil sie es *haben* besuchen können.	Now they can recommend the restaurant because they have been able to visit it.

EXERCISE

K   Put the following sentences into German.

1   She wants to see the menu.

2   I would like to see the wine list.

3   They must pay by credit card.

4   I can recommend the restaurant.

5   We will go to the café at 3.30.

6   I'll have a taxi ordered.

7   The café is nice, because you can read newspapers there.

8   It's good because we have been able to reserve a table.

3.10 *Word order and phrasal verbs*

Nouns which are used with a verb in a set phrase are treated similarly to separable prefixes, and are put at the end of main clauses. Examples are:

Phrase	Meaning
Geburtstag haben	to have a birthday
Glück haben	to be lucky

Phrase	Meaning
Pech haben	to be unlucky
unter Druck setzen	to put under pressure
zur Verfügung haben	to have at one's disposal/available
zur Verfügung stellen	to put at sb's disposal

PHRASAL VERBS: WORD ORDER RULES

Rule	Example	Meaning
Noun goes at the end in a main clause	Das stellte mich dann unter *Druck*.	That then put me under pressure.
	Ich habe am 20. März *Geburtstag*.	My birthday is on 20 March.
	Wir haben viele Videos zur *Verfügung*.	We have many videos available.
Subordinate clauses – noun comes immediately before the verb at end of clause	Das war, weil ich ihn unter *Druck* setzte.	That was because I was putting him under pressure.

EXERCISE

L   Put the following sentences into German.

1   When is your birthday?

2   They put him under pressure.

3   I know when his birthday is.

4   They said that they have a lot of videos available.

5   They have been lucky today.

3.11 *Positioning* nicht *and negative elements*

Nicht (not), *nie* (never) and *kaum* (scarcely) make statements negative.

Rule	Example	Meaning
nicht/nie/kaum normally go after a noun object	Ich kenne die Leute *nicht*.	I don't know the people.
	Ich habe ihn *kaum* gesehen.	I have hardly seen him.
nicht/nie/kaum normally go before a verb complement (e.g. place phrase) and before the past participle	Wir sind *nicht* nach Dresden gefahren.	We did not go to Dresden.
	Er ist *nie* in den Niederlanden gewesen.	He has never been to the Netherlands.

Rule	Example	Meaning
nicht/nie comes before an adverb of manner	Sie haben das *nicht* richtig interpretiert. Ich habe es *nie* völlig verstanden.	You did not interpret that correctly. I never completely understood it.

EXERCISE

M   Insert the negative element in each sentence.

1   Ich habe Drogen genommen. (nicht)

2   Sie hat sehr viel geraucht. (nie)

3   Er hat die Drogenprobleme richtig analysiert. (nicht)

4   Die Frau hat Heroin genommen. (nie)

5   Sie ist zur Drogenberatungsstelle gegangen. (nicht)

6   Viele haben ganz aufgehört, Drogen zu nehmen. (nicht)

3.12 *Time, manner and place adverb rules*

Rule	Example	Meaning
Time phrases *then* manner phrases *then* place phrases	Ich fahre morgen mit dem Bus. Ich fahre mit dem Bus nach Leipzig. Sie fliegen um 15.30 mit Lufthansa nach Paris.	I am going tomorrow by bus. I am going by bus to Leipzig. At 15.30 they are flying with Lufthansa to Paris.
Put one adverb at the start of a clause or sentence to avoid having three adverbs or adverbial phrases in a row	Morgen fahren wir mit dem Bus nach Kiel. Nächste Woche fliegen wir mit Lufthansa nach Rom.	Tomorrow we are going by bus to Kiel. Next week we are flying to Rome with Lufthansa.

EXERCISE

N   Insert the adverbs and adverbial phrases in the correct order.

1   Sie fährt. (nach Genf; am Montag)

2   Er fliegt. (am Donnerstag; mit British Airways)

3   Wir wandern. (in den Alpen; den ganzen Tag)

4   Meine Kusine kommt. (vom Bahnhof; mit dem Taxi)

5   Sie reist. (nach Italien; zu Weihnachten; mit der Bahn)

3.13 *Order of nouns and pronouns*

There are fixed rules on the order of nouns and pronouns.

Rule	Example	Meaning
Pronouns precede nouns	Wir gaben es dem Mann.	We gave it to the man.
	Wir liehen ihnen die Kassetten.	We lent them the cassettes.
If there are two pronouns, Accusative pronoun precedes Dative pronoun	Wir brachten sie ihm.	We brought them to him.
	Ich gab es ihnen.	I gave it to them.
If there are two nouns, the Dative noun precedes the Accusative noun	Ich überreichte der Frau die Papiere.	I handed the papers over to the woman.

EXERCISE

O Give the German for the following sentences.

1   We sent them the flowers.

2   I gave them to my mother.

3   She gave the book to her husband.

4   He lent it to his friend.

5   She gave the book back to him.

6   I sent it to them.

7   They showed him the book.

8   He showed them the plans.

9   They gave the manager the watch.

10   We sold the car to our friends.

3.14 *Finding the subject*

In order to understand a German sentence it is vital to establish what the subject is.

Here is a reminder of the forms of the definite article. (See Chapter 6 for more on Articles.)

DEFINITE ARTICLE

	M	F	N	Pl
Nom.	der	die	das	die
Acc.	den	die	das	die
Dat.	dem	der	dem	den
Gen.	des	der	des	der

The subject of a sentence is Nominative. A noun preceded by a preposition cannot be the subject. There may be a 'dummy' subject, *es*, which anticipates the actual subject, e.g. *Es* waren viele Wolken am Himmel. *Es* ist gestern etwas Schreckliches passiert.

Rule	Example
Subject may be a noun or a noun and determiner(s)	*Die Frau* wohnt in Moskau. *Diese kranke Frau* ist meine Schwester.
Subject may be a noun followed by a relative clause	*Die Frau, die seit vielen Jahren bei SAP arbeitet,* ist gestorben.
The subject may be a whole clause	*Dass es kompliziert ist,* ist ganz klar.
The subject may be a phrase including an infinitive	*Das Problem zu verstehen* verlangt viel Insider-Wissen.

EXERCISES

P Look at each sentence and say whether the student is the subject of the sentence or not.

1 Ich ging mit der Studentin in die Stadt.

2 Die Studentin hat die Arbeit gut gemacht.

3 Ich habe die Studentin nicht gesehen.

4 Das ist für die Studentin.

5 Die Studentin sehen sie jeden Tag.

Q   Underline the subject in each of the following sentences.

1   Den Managern haben sie die Informationen gegeben.

2   Mit den Maschinen hatten sie immer Probleme.

3   Die Abteilungsleiterin fanden sie alle sehr sympathisch.

4   Es ist relativ leicht, die Probleme zu verstehen.

5   Den Journalisten haben sie interessant gefunden.

6   Aus vielen Gründen kann das Projekt problematisch werden.

7   Gegenüber vom Eingang steht der Leiter des Büros.

8   Nach den letzten Tagen kann man nicht mehr von einem guten Manager sprechen.

9   Einen Monat lang kam keine Nachricht von ihr.

10   Trotz der Schwierigkeiten haben sie es gut gemacht.

4 Numbers and statistics

4.1 Cardinal numbers

German numbers look very long when written, but are rarely written out in full. When noting numbers 20–99 it may help to write the digit first, then the higher number. e.g. neunundzwanzig = you hear 9 first, so write it down, 9, then you hear 20, so write a 2 to the left of the 9, = 29!

Rule	Example	Exception
For negative numbers use *minus*	−5,3% (spoken as *minus* 5 Komma drei Prozent)	
0 = *null*	0,5 = null Komma fünf	
1 = use *eins* if not followed by a noun	das ist Nummer eins	
1 = use indefinite article if followed by a noun	wir haben einen Mercedes	es ist ein Uhr = it's 1.00 (es ist eine Uhr = it's a clock/watch)
1–12 are simple numbers	zwei, drei, elf	2 = on the phone use *zwo*, avoids confusion with *drei*
13–19 = digit + *zehn*	fünfzehn, achtzehn	sechzehn, siebzehn

Rule	Example	Exception
20–90 = all multiples of ten up to 90 end in -zig	zwanzig, vierzig, fünfzig	dreißig; note spelling of sechzig and siebzig
21–29, 31–49, etc. einund-, zweiund-, etc.	einundzwanzig neununddreißig	
100–199 = lower number comes after hundert	hunderteins hundertzweiundzwanzig	numbers including 100 = use einhundert e.g. zweitausendeinhundert
200–1000 = number of hundreds + extra number	dreihunderteins vierhundertzwanzig	
1,000 2,110	tausend zweitausendeinhundertzehn	
1,000,000	eine Million	
1,000,000,000	eine Milliarde	

EXERCISE

A Write down the next number in the series.

1 drei, sechs, neun

2 zehn, zwanzig, dreißig

3 fünfundzwanzig, zwanzig, fünfzehn

4 zweiundzwanzig, dreiunddreißig, vierundvierzig

5 zwanzig, neunzehn, achtzehn

4.2 *Ordinal numbers*

Ordinal numbers are treated like other adjectives and have appropriate endings.

Rule	Example	Exception
The 1st, 2nd, 3rd, etc. = use definite article + ordinal	der erste, etc. (all forms decline) Das Zimmer ist im ersten Stock.	
Formation 2nd–19th = add -te to cardinal numbers	der zweite	der dritte der siebte, der achte
20th–100th = add -ste to cardinal numbers	der vierundzwanzigste der hundertste	
Ordinals can be combined with superlatives	der zweitbeste (second best), drittbeste, viertbeste, etc.	

Rule	Example	Exception
Centuries = use *im* + ordinal number + full stop + *Jahrhundert*	im 19. (spoken n*eunzehnten*) Jahrhundert	
Dates use *am* + ordinal number + full stop + month	am 5. März	
Titles are written in full	Elisabeth die Zweite Karl der Erste	

EXERCISE

B How do you say the following in German?

1 My office is on the 5th floor. (das Büro)

2 It's the second best result this year. (das Ergebnis)

3 The Trade Fair begins on 3rd January. (die Messe)

4 The film is about advertising in the twentieth century. (die Werbung)

4.3 *Number phrases and expressions*

A pair; a few	ein Paar; ein paar
A dozen; a hundred	ein Dutzend; ein Hundert
Several hundred; a few thousand	einige Hundert; einige Tausend
Thousands; millions	Tausende; Millionen

English	Rule	Example
Number of times	Add *-mal* to number (except *einmal* once)	zweimal (twice) zwölfmal (twelve times)
Number of kinds of sth	Add *-erlei* to number	einerlei, zweierlei, fünferlei
Duration or age	Add umlaut + *-ig* to time phrase	viertägig (lasting 4 days) dreistündig, zweiwöchig einjährig (lasting one year, or one-year-old) BUT sechsmonatig (for 6 months or 6-month-old)
Regular times	Add umlaut + *lich* to time phrase	stündlich (hourly) täglich (daily) wöchentlich, jährlich BUT monatlich (monthly)

English	Rule	Example
Dates, e.g. 1910	Spoken '19 + hundert + 10' (not 'one thousand nine hundred and ten')	neunzehnhundertzehn
1930s, 1940s, etc.	Cardinal number + er (adj. never changes) + *Jahre*	die 30er Jahre in den dreißiger Jahren
At the beginning, middle and ends of periods of time	'At the' omitted in German before *Anfang, Mitte* and *Ende* + years, decades and centuries	Anfang 1999 Ende der dreißiger Jahre Mitte des 19. Jahrhunderts

EXERCISE

C Insert the correct word(s) in each sentence.

1 Es gibt _____ Regionen. (two kinds of)

2 Sie investierten _____ so viel in die Infrastruktur. (3 times)

3 Sie sind jetzt _____ attraktiver als vorher. (6 times)

4 _____ mussten viele Arbeiter neue Stellen finden. (at the end of the 1990s)

5 _____ Städte arbeiten eng zusammen. (a dozen)

6 _____ exportierte die Firma viel nach Frankreich. (in the middle of the 1990s)

4.4 *Days, dates and time phrases*

PREPOSITIONS AND TIME PHRASES

Preposition	Rule	Example
am	With days With parts of the day With dates	*am* Sonntag *am* Sonntagnachmittag *am* 5. Dezember
am	With days of the week + Accusative case for date	*am* Donnerstag, den 13. Juni
im	With years With months/seasons	*im* 1999 *im* Dezember/Frühling
um	At + clock times At + noon and midnight	*um* fünf Uhr *um* Mitternacht/um Mittag

DATES

Rule	Example
es ist/heute ist + Nominative date	es ist der 5. Januar heute ist Montag, der 5. Januar
wir haben + Accusative date	wir haben Dienstag, den 18. März
Accusative date at the head of a letter normally follows the town/city	Dresden, den 21. April

EXERCISE

D   Put the following sentences into German.

1   The press conference is on the 21st April. (die Pressekonferenz)

2   The demonstration is on Wednesday afternoon. (die Demonstration)

3   The election is on Thursday the 14th February. (die Wahl)

4   The debate is at noon. (die Debatte)

5   The Russian Revolution was at the beginning of the 20th century. (die Russische Revolution)

KEY DATES LISTED CHRONOLOGICALLY

English term	German term
Carnival Monday	Rosenmontag
Ash Wednesday	Aschermittwoch
Easter	Ostern
Easter Monday	Ostermontag
Corpus Christi	Fronleichnam
Whitsun	Pfingsten
Ascension	Christi Himmelfahrt
Ascension of the Virgin Mary	Maria Himmelfahrt
3.10 (Reunification of Germany)	Tag der Einheit
All Saints	Allerheiligen
Christmas	Weihnachten
New Year	Sylvester

There are a few set phrases using these times of year. Where the day of the week or a day is mentioned you use *am*, otherwise use *zu*.

English	German
On Ash Wednesday	am Aschermittwoch
On Easter Monday	am Ostermontag
At Christmas	zu Weihnachten
At Easter	zu Ostern
At New Year	zu Neujahr
At Whitsun	zu Pfingsten

EXERCISE

E Answer the following questions with a German phrase using *am* or *zu*.

1 Wann gibt es Ostereier?

2 Wann bekommen viele Kinder Geschenke, auch wenn sie nicht Geburtstag haben?

3 Wann gibt es in Deutschland Feuerwerke?

4 Wann fangen Christen an zu fasten?

5 Wann feiert man die Wiedervereinigung?

CLOCK TIMES

Rule	Example	Exception
nach = past the hour *vor* = before the hour	fünf nach vier = 4.05 Viertel vor sieben = 6.45	halb fünf, halb sieben, etc. = 4.30, 6.30, etc.
Number + *Uhr* = o'clock	sieben Uhr = 7.00	ein Uhr; eins = 1.00

Time	morgens/nachmittags/ abends	00.01 –12.00	12.01 –24.00
2.00	zwei Uhr	zwei Uhr	vierzehn Uhr
2.05	fünf nach zwei	zwei Uhr fünf	vierzehn Uhr fünf
2.15	Viertel nach zwei	zwei Uhr fünfzehn	vierzehn Uhr fünfzehn
2.30	halb drei	zwei Uhr dreißig	vierzehn Uhr dreißig
2.35	fünfundzwanzig vor drei	zwei Uhr fünfunddreißig	vierzehn Uhr fünfunddreißig
2.45	Viertel vor drei	zwei Uhr fünfundvierzig	vierzehn Uhr fünfundvierzig
2.55	fünf vor drei	zwei Uhr fünfundfünfzig	vierzehn Uhr fünfundfünfzig

USEFUL TIME PHRASES

auf die Dauer	in the long run
bis vor kurzem	until recently
es war einmal	once upon a time
in den vergangenen Monaten	in the past months
in letzter Zeit	recently
seit Jahresbeginn	since the start of the year
erstens, zweitens, schließlich	firstly, secondly, finally
erst Anfang Januar	not until the start of January
erst nächste Woche	not until next week
erst am Montag	not until Monday
erst um Mittag	not until midday
erst später	not until later
Tag für Tag	day by day

EXERCISE

F   Days, dates and time phrases. Give the German for the following.

1   in 1989

2   not until midnight

3   until recently

4   at the start of October

5   at the end of January

6   in autumn

7   day by day

8   It was on Wednesday 30th January.

9   in the long run

10   on Saturday afternoon

11   7.30am

12   in winter

13   in the 1920s

14   22.55

15   recently

16   There is one cathedral and there are four museums.

17   There are hundreds of bars.

18   There are dozens of cafés.

19   There are millions.

20   My birthday is on the 29th June.

4.5 *Quantities, prices and statistics*

In German you do not need a word for 'of' when talking about quantities of food and drink. Use the table to order, taking one item from each column.

ich möchte	einen Becher	Chips
ich hätte gern	einen Liter	Joghurt
	einen Beutel	Kaffee
	eine Dose	Käse
	eine Flasche	Marmelade
	eine Packung	Wein
	eine Tüte	Tomaten
	ein Pfund	Kirschen
	ein halbes Pfund	
	drei Pfund	
	ein Kilo	
	zwei Kilo	
	ein Glas	

EXERCISE

G   Translate the following sentences into German.

1   I would like a bag of crisps.

2   I would like a tin of tomatoes.

3   I would like a litre of wine.

4   I would like half a pound of cherries.

5   I would like a jar of jam.

PRICES: USE THE PRICE FOLLOWED BY THE NOMINATIVE CASE

e.g. Es kostet DM3 das Kilo.

Es kostet DM5 der Liter.

English	German
10 pence a pound	zehn Pfennig das Pfund
DM 7.99 a litre	sieben Mark neunundneunzig der Liter
ÖS 10 per kilo	zehn Schillinge pro Kilo
SF 2 a bottle	zwei Franken die Flasche

FRACTIONS

half	die Hälfte
half of the people	die Hälfte der Leute
half an apple	ein halber Apfel
half a bottle	eine halbe Flasche
a third	ein Drittel
a quarter	ein Viertel
a tenth	ein Zehntel
two thirds	zwei Drittel
1½, 2½, 3½	anderthalb, zweieinhalb, dreieinhalb

PERCENTAGES

English	Written German	Spoken German
1.5%	1,5%	eins Komma fünf Prozent
25.6%	25,6%	fünfundzwanzig Komma sechs Prozent
2,000% (comma after 2)	2.000 (full stop after 2) Prozent or 2 000 (space after 2) Prozent	zweitausend Prozent
Fell/rose by 10%	sanken/stiegen um 10%	sanken/stiegen um zehn Prozent
Round about 5%	um die 5%	um die fünf Prozent

EXERCISE

H Give the German for the following number phrases.

1 Die Temperatur stieg (by 2%).

2 (Half the people) leidet unter den Emissionen.

3 (Two thirds of the people) nehmen ihre Flaschen zum Altglascontainer.

4 Die Umweltverschmutzung in dieser Region ist (by 2%) gesunken.

5 (72.5%) fahren mit dem Auto zur Arbeit.

5

Nouns

Contents

5.1 Gender rules

5.2 Nouns with more than one gender, each with a different meaning

5.3 Gender of compound nouns

5.4 Singular/plural nouns

5.5 Formation of plurals

5.6 Declining nouns

5.7 Weak nouns

5.8 Adjectival nouns

5.9 Nouns in apposition

5.1 *Gender rules*

It is possible to have a good idea of what gender a noun is in German. This section of the chapter gives guidelines on gender by formation, and then gender according to meaning. In each section the rules relate to masculine, feminine and neuter nouns in that order.

GENDER BY FORMATION: MASCULINE

Ending	Example	Exception
-ant, -ent	Diamant, Präsident	
-är	Millionär	
-ast	Palast	
-er (people and machines)	Lehrer, Computer	not many: Butter (f), Steuer (f), Fenster (nt), Fieber (nt)

Ending	Example	Exception
-ich, -ig	Teppich, König	
-ismus, -ist	Pessimismus, Optimist	
-ling	Lehrling (apprentice)	
-or	Professor	very few; Labor (nt)

GENDER BY FORMATION: FEMININE

Ending	Example	Exception
-ei	Bäckerei	very, very few; Ei (nt)
-heit	Freiheit	
-ie	Energie	
-ik	Politik	
-in	Polizistin	very, very few; Nikotin (nt)
-ion	Nation	
-keit	Freundlichkeit	
-schaft	Freundschaft	
-tät	Nationalität	
-ung	Hoffnung	

GENDER BY FORMATION: NEUTER

Ending	Example	Exception
-chen	Brötchen	
-ett	Etikett	
-lein	Fräulein	
-ma	Dogma	very few; Firma (f)
-nis (70 per cent neuter – 30 per cent feminine)	Hindernis	Erlaubnis (f)
-on	Telefon	
-tum	Fürstentum	Irrtum (m) mistake; Reichtum (m)
-um	Museum, Studium	

EXERCISE

A Insert the correct definite article in each sentence.

1 Wo ist _____ Zentrum?

2 _____ Museum ist neben dem Dom.

3 _____ Bücherei ist in der Stadtmitte.

4 _____ Lehrerin arbeitet in der Stadt.

5 Wo ist _____ Universität?

As well as rules for gender by formation there are rules which relate to gender by meaning. These help you decide if a noun is masculine, feminine or neuter.

GENDER BY MEANING: MASCULINE

Meaning	Example	Exception
Day, month, season	Montag, Januar, Herbst	
Points of compass	Norden, Südwesten	
Male people and animals	Bruder, Tiger	very, very few; Baby (nt)
Types of weather	Schnee, Frost, Nebel, Regen, Wind	Sonne (f), Eis (nt) Gewitter (nt)
Rivers	Main, Rhein	Donau (f), Elbe (f), Mosel (f), Oder (f), Weser (f)
Makes of cars	Porsche, Mercedes	

GENDER BY MEANING: FEMININE

Meaning	Example	Exception
Female people and animals	Schwester, Katze	very, very few: Mädchen (nt), Baby (nt), Fräulein (nt)
German rivers	Donau, Elbe, Mosel, Oder, Weser	Main (m), Rhein (m)
Motorbikes, planes, ships	Honda, Boeing, Titanic	

GENERED BY MEANING: NEUTER

Meaning	Example	Exception
Countries	Italien	relatively few; Türkei (f), Schweiz (f), BRD (f), USA (pl), Niederlande (pl)
Towns	Berlin, Hamburg	
Continents	Afrika, Amerika, Asien	
Metals	Eisen, Gold, Silber	Stahl (m), Bronze (f)
Young humans and animals	Baby, Kalb, Lamm	

EXERCISE

B   Give the gender of each word and explain your choice.

1   Elefant

2   Europa

3   Frankreich

4   Gold

5   Lamm

6   Nebel

7   Oktober

8   Rhein

9   Süden

10   Tante

5.2 *Nouns with more than one gender, each with a different meaning*

There are relatively few nouns with two genders. The following are the most common. Context usually makes the meaning clear anyway.

Noun	Masc.	Fem.	Neut.
Band	volume		tape, ribbon
Erbe	heir		inheritance
Golf	gulf		golf
Heide	heathen	heathland	

Noun	Masc.	Fem.	Neut.
Kiefer	jaw	pine tree	
Leiter	leader	ladder	
Pony	fringe (of hair)		pony
See	lake	sea	
Tor	fool		gate, door
Weise	wise man	way, manner	

EXERCISE

C   Revise the nouns which can have two different genders and meanings and translate these sentences into English.

    1   Das Brandenburger Tor ist für viele das Symbol Berlins.

    2   Der Weise weiß alles über die Geschichte Berlins.

    3   Der Leiter der Gruppe kommt aus einem Berliner Vorort.

    4   Wo kann man in Berlin Golf spielen?

    5   Auf der Heide findet man viele Blumen, die man in Berlin nicht sieht.

5.3 *Gender of compound nouns*

Compound nouns have the gender and plural of the last element. (See Chapter 1.)

EXERCISE

D   Give the gender of each of the following compound nouns and explain your choice.

    e.g. Milchmann   *Masc. 'Mann' is a male person*

    1   Atomenergie

    2   Bundesministerium

    3   Innenminister

    4   Politiklehrerin

    5   Friedenspolitik

5.4 *Singular/plural nouns*

Some nouns are singular in German, plural in English.

German – singular noun	English – plural noun
das Archiv	archives
die Brille	spectacles
das Fernglas	binoculars
die Hose	trousers
der Inhalt	contents
der Lohn	wages
das Mittelalter	Middle Ages
die Politik	politics
die Schere	scissors
die Treppe	stairs
die Umgebung	surroundings
die Waage	scales
die Wahl	elections

Some nouns are plural in German, singular in English.

German – plural noun	English – singular noun
die Lebensmittel	food
die Möbel	furniture
die Zinsen	interest (on a loan)

EXERCISE

E   Insert the correct form of the Present tense of the verb in each sentence.

1   Die Brille _____ auf dem Tisch. (liegen)

2   Lebensmittel _____ hier sehr teuer. (sein)

3   Die Möbel _____ alle aus Schweden. (sein)

4   Ihre Hose _____ sehr elegant _____. (aussehen)

5   Die Zinsen _____ leider sehr hoch. (sein)

6   Die Wahl _____ am Montag _____. (stattfinden)

5.5 *Formation of plurals*

The following rules should help in forming plurals. The most common plural forms are given first.

MASCULINE NOUNS: PLURALS

Rule	Usefulness	Examples
Plural same as singular	Almost all nouns ending in -el, -en, -er	Onkel, Computer
Plural adds umlaut to stressed vowel	About 20 nouns only	Apfel, Boden, Bruder, Garten, Hafen, Laden, Mangel, Mantel, Nagel, Ofen, Schaden, Schwager, Vater, Vogel
Add -er	Less than 10 in total	Geist, Ski
Add umlaut + er	Less than 10 in total	Gott, Irrtum (error), Mann, Wald, Wurm
Add -e	Most other masculine nouns	Arm, Beruf, Besuch, Erfolg, Hund, Monat, Mond, Schuh, Stoff, Tag, Verlag, Verlust, Versuch
Add umlaut + -e	About half the nouns which could have umlaut do so	Fuß, Kanal, Stuhl
Add -en, -n	A few irregular nouns; weak masculine nouns	Gedanke, Mensch, Name, Professor, Schmerz, See, Staat, Student
Add -s	Very rare, mostly 'foreign' words	Balkon, Chef, Ossi (ex. DDR citizen), Park, Scheck, Streik, Wessi (W. German)

FEMININE NOUNS: PLURALS

These are the easiest. The great majority add -*n* or -*en*.

Rule	Usefulness	Examples
Add -n, -en	Over 90 per cent	Arbeit
Add umlaut + -e	About 25 per cent of one syllable nouns	Angst, Bank, Frucht, Hand, Kraft, Kuh, Kunst, Laus, Luft, Macht, Maus, Nacht, Not, Nuss, Stadt, Wand, Wurst
Add -nen	All fem. nouns ending -in	Studentin
Add -se	All fem. nouns ending -nis	Kenntnis
Add umlaut	Only two	Mutter, Tochter
Add -s	Only two common ones	Kamera, Oma

NEUTER NOUNS: PLURALS

Rule	Usefulness	Examples
Plural same as singular	All nouns ending in -el, -n, -er, -chen, -lein	Messer, Mädchen
Add -er	Fair number of neut. nouns	Gesicht, Kind
Add umlaut + er	Many monosyllabic nouns	Blatt, Dorf, Tal
Add -e	About 75 per cent of neut. nouns	Jahr, Verbot
Add -se	All neut. nouns ending -nis	Geheimnis
Add -en, -n	Very few nouns	Auge, Bett, Ende, Hemd, Herz, Insekt, Interesse, Ohr, Verb
Add -s	Very rare; mostly 'foreign' nouns	Atelier, Auto, Baby, Café, Hotel, Restaurant, Sofa

IRREGULAR PLURALS

Although irregular, these plural rules are very useful, as they are very reliable.

Rule	Singular	Plural
-a > -en	Pizza, Villa	Pizzen (also Pizzas), Villen
-al > -ien	Material, Mineral	Materialien, Mineralien
-ma > -en	Drama, Firma, Thema	Dramen, Firmen, Themen
-mann > -leute	Fachmann (expert)	Fachleute
-o > -en	Risiko	Risiken
-um > -en	Museum	Museen
-us > -en	Rhythmus	Rhythmen

EXERCISE

F   Rewrite the sentences, making the italicized nouns and their verbs plural.

1   Das *Atelier* liegt in der Stadtmitte.

2   Das *Interesse* der Gruppe ist an der EU.

3   Das *Risiko* ist groß.

4   Der *Chef* fliegt oft in die USA.

5   Der *Computer* ist 4 Jahre alt.

6   Der *Erfolg* der Projekte ist klar.

7   Der *Hafen* ist international bekannt.

8   Der *Mann* arbeitet bei einer Software-Firma.

9   Der *Name* war weltbekannt.

10   Der *Streik* hat nicht lange gedauert.

11   Die *Firma* hat ihren Hauptsitz in Bayern.

12   Die *Stadt* ist multikulturell.

5.6 *Declining nouns*

Rule	Example	Exception
Masc. + Neut. Sing. nouns add -s or -es in Genitive Sing.	des Bahnhofs am Ende des Jahres	all weak nouns
Nouns add -n in Dative Plural if they don't already end in -n	mit den Kindern	plural nouns ending in **-s** do not add -n, e.g. mit den Autos
Masc. weak nouns (see below) add -n, or -en in all cases except Nom. Sing.	Astronaut, Franzose, Herr, Mensch, Polizist	

5.7 *Weak nouns*

All weak nouns are masculine. They are unusual in that they add *-n* or *-en* in all cases except the Nominative Singular. They are relatively easy to recognize.

Rule	Example
A few nouns ending in -e	Bote, Chinese, Franzose, Schwede
All foreign nouns ending in -ant, -aut	Diamant, Astronaut
All foreign nouns ending in -ist, -ent, -krat	Polizist, Dissident, Aristokrat
A few nouns ending in consonants	Bauer, Fürst, Held, Herr, Mensch, Nachbar
Five weak masculine nouns have the ending -n in the Accusative and Dative Singular and -ns in the Genitive Singular (e.g., der Glaube, des Glaubens)	Glaube, Wille, Buchstabe, Gedanke, Name

WEAK MASCULINE NOUNS: DECLENSION

	Add -n	Add -en
Nom. Sing.	der Franzose	der Polizist
Acc. Sing.	den Franzosen	den Polizisten
Dat. Sing.	dem Franzosen	dem Polizisten
Gen. Sing.	des Franzosen	des Polizisten
Nom./Acc. Plural	die Franzosen	die Polizisten
Dat. Plural	den Franzosen	den Polizisten
Gen. Plural	der Franzosen	der Polizisten

EXERCISE

G   Give the correct form of each noun (in brackets).

1   Am Anfang des (Jahr) kamen viele Asylsuchende nach Deutschland.

2   Nach einigen (Jahr) haben sie sich in der Stadt etabliert.

3   Für den (Optimist) ist das Leben in einem neuen Land immer schön.

4   Jeder will einen netten (Nachbar) haben.

5   Die Zahl der (Arbeitslose) ist in letzter Zeit gestiegen.

5.8 *Adjectival nouns*

Adjectives can be used as nouns. They are written with a capital letter and have the normal appropriate adjective endings. Past or present participles can be used as Adjectival nouns, e.g. *der Angestellte, der Erwachsene, der Reisende* (see Chapter 8). The table shows the endings of male adjectival nouns. Check Chapter 8 if you cannot remember the feminine and neuter endings.

ADJECTIVAL NOUNS: DECLENSION

	Weak endings	Mixed endings	Strong endings
Nom. Sing.	der Arbeitslose	ein Arbeitsloser	Arbeitsloser
Acc. Sing.	den Arbeitslosen	einen Arbeitslosen	Arbeitslosen
Dat. Sing.	dem Arbeitslosen	einem Arbeitslosen	Arbeitslosem
Gen. Sing.	des Arbeitslosen	eines Arbeitslosen	Arbeitslosen
Nom. Plural	die Arbeitslosen	keine Arbeitslosen	Arbeitslose

	Weak endings	**Mixed endings**	**Strong endings**
Acc. Plural	die Arbeitslosen	keine Arbeitslosen	Arbeitslose
Dat. Plural	den Arbeitslosen	keinen Arbeitslosen	Arbeitslosen
Gen. Plural	der Arbeitslosen	keiner Arbeitslosen	Arbeitsloser

Rule	**Example**	**Meaning**
Weak endings	Die Arbeitslosen sind oft deprimiert. Der Verwundete ist da.	The unemployed people are often depressed. The wounded man is there.
Mixed endings	Keine Erwachsenen waren anwesend. Für einen Erwachsenen ist das Buch uninteressant.	No adults were present. The book is not of interest to an adult.
Strong endings	Alle Angestellten feiern. Arbeitsloser Max Niemann gewann DM500.	All the employees are celebrating. Max Niemann, an unemployed man, won DM500.

EXERCISE

H   Insert the correct form of these adjectival nouns.

1   Für viele (Erwachsene) ist Weihnachten weniger interessant.

2   Meine (Bekannte) feiern am 1. Weihnachtstag.

3   Bei vielen (Arbeitslose) spielt Alhohol eine Rolle.

4   Einige (Deutsche) fahren dreimal im Jahr auf Urlaub.

5   Die Hauptprobleme der (Obdachlose) haben mit der Gesundheit zu tun.

5.9 *Nouns in apposition*

A noun phrase in apposition comes immediately after a noun and gives more information about it. It is in the same case as the noun.

Rule	**Example**	**Meaning**
Nominative case	Das ist Herr Hornburg, mein Chef.	This is Mr Hornburg, my boss.
Accusative case	Das ist für Herrn Hornburg, meinen Chef.	That is for my boss, Mr Hornburg.
Dative case	Meine Universität ist in Regensburg, einer Stadt an der Donau.	My university is in Regensburg, a town on the Danube.

Nouns in apposition are found most commonly in expressions involving places and quantities (see Chapter 4). No word is needed for the English 'of'.

	Example	Meaning
Places	Die Insel Wangerooge ist an der Nordseeküste.	The island of Wangerooge is on the North Sea coast.
	die Universität München	the University of Munich
Measurement	Ein Kilo Äpfel kostet DM3.	A kilo of apples costs DM3.
Quantity	Ich kaufte eine Flasche Rotwein.	I bought a bottle of red wine.

EXERCISE

I   Insert the correct form of the nouns in apposition.

    I   Er ging mit seinen Kollegen, (the teachers), zur Demonstration.

    2   Er lebte in einer 2-Zimmer-Wohnung, (a flat) am Stadtrande.

    3   Wir kauften Möbel für meinen Untermieter, (a student).

    4   Das ist die Hauptindustrie in Schwerin, (the capital) des Landes Mecklenburg-Vorpommern.

Articles

6.1 Definite article and its use

The definite article 'the' changes in German according to gender, number and case of the noun it goes with. Its use is not identical to that in English.

	M	F	N	Pl
Nom.	der	die	das	die
Acc.	den	die	das	die
Dat.	dem	der	dem	den
Gen.	des	der	des	der

USE OF DEFINITE ARTICLE

Rule	Example	Exception
Use to refer to something specific	Die Musik ist herrlich. (The music is wonderful.)	
Use for abstract nouns, gives idea of something as a whole (no article in English)	Das Leben ist schön.	Musik ist herrlich. (All music is wonderful.)

Rule	Example	Exception
Use for parts of the body; English uses possessive 'my'	Ich wasche mir die Haare. (I wash my hair) Der Kopf tut mir weh. (my head hurts)	You can also say 'ich wasche meine Haare' You can also say 'mein Kopf tut weh'
Use for feminine and plural countries	Er besucht die Schweiz. Sie wohnen in den USA.	
Use for streets (no article in English)	Sie wohnt in der Waldstraße.	
Use with prepositions + days	Ich komme am Freitag.	
Use with prepositions + months/seasons	Ich habe im Dezember Geburtstag. Wir fahren im Frühling.	Definite article is not always used after *seit* and *vor*, e.g. Sie ist seit September da. Sie machen es vor Januar.
Use for meals (no article in English)	Das Mittagessen ist fertig.	
Use for prices/quantities (indefinite article in English)	Das kostet DM2 das Kilo.	
Use for proper names preceded by an adjective (no article in English) Use with proper names if used dismissively/familiarly	die alte Frau Schmidt (old Mrs Smith) Der Peter hat immer Probleme. (roughly: that guy Peter always has problems)	
Use in set phrases	in die Stadt fahren (to go into town) mit dem Bus/Taxi/Zug (by bus/taxi/train)	zu Fuß (on foot)

EXERCISE

A Translate the following sentences into German.

1 The doctor is from the Czech Republic.

2 He lives in Station Road.

3 He went to town.

4 He went by bus to Cologne.

5 He broke his leg.

6   His brother lives in the USA.

7   He is coming to Germany in the spring.

8   His sister has been living in Aachen since April.

9   Her operation is on Wednesday.

10   Grapes cost DM4 a pound.

6.2 *Indefinite article and its use*

The indefinite article is used for 'a'. It changes in German according to gender, number and case of the noun it goes with. Its use is not identical to that in English.

	M	F	N	Pl
Nom.	ein	eine	ein	–
Acc.	einen	eine	ein	–
Dat.	einem	einer	einem	–
Gen.	eines	einer	eines	–

NEGATIVE INDEFINITE ARTICLE AND USE

The word *kein* corresponds to 'not a'. The endings are identical to 'ein' in the singular. (the endings of the possessive determiners *mein, dein,* etc. are identical to those of *kein*).

	M	F	N	Pl
Nom.	kein	keine	kein	keine
Acc.	keinen	keine	kein	keine
Dat.	keinem	keiner	keinem	keinen
Gen.	keines	keiner	keines	keiner

EXERCISE

B   Insert the correct form of *ein* or *kein*.

1   Heute hat (_____) Frau mehr Möglichkeiten als vor 100 Jahren. (ein)

2   Auch wenn sie (_____) Familie hat, kann sie weiterarbeiten. (ein)

3   Eine Frau mit (_____) guten Stelle kann viel verdienen. (ein)

4   In einer idealen Welt gibt es (_____) Diskriminierung. (kein)

5   Es gibt (_____) Grund, Frauen weniger Geld für die gleiche Arbeit zu geben. (kein)

6.3 *Omission of article*

Rule	Example	Exception
Omitted in preposition phrases where English has an article	zu Ende (at an end)	
Omitted after verb 'to be' or 'to become'	Er ist Mechaniker. Sie wird Ärztin.	Use article when the noun is qualified. Er ist *ein* guter Mechaniker.
Omitted after *als* = as	Ich spreche als Schottin. (as a Scotswoman) Sie arbeitet als Kellnerin. (she's working as a waitress)	Use article when the noun is qualified. Ich spreche als *eine* geborene Schottin. (as a woman born in Scotland)
Omitted in certain time phrases (use article in English)	Es ist Viertel vor eins. (it is a quarter to one)	
Omitted in a few set phrases (use article in English)	Es ist Geschmackssache. (it's a matter of taste)	
Omitted in expressions about pains	Ich habe Kopfschmerzen. (I have a headache)	Ich habe einen Kater. (I have a hangover)

EXERCISE

C   Translate the following sentences into German.

1   I have a headache.

2   That was a matter of taste.

3   Work finishes at a quarter to five.

4   I work as a nurse.

5   She is a dentist.

6   It is at an end.

7   She is speaking as a doctor.

8   She is a good doctor.

6.4 *Demonstrative article*

Dieser corresponds to 'this' in English. It is used before nouns. It changes in German according to gender, number and case of the noun it goes with.

	M	F	N	Pl
Nom.	dieser	diese	dieses	diese
Acc.	diesen	diese	dieses	diese
Dat.	diesem	dieser	diesem	diesen
Gen.	dieses	dieser	dieses	dieser

EXERCISE

D Insert the correct form of *dieser*.

I _____ Wetter ist ungewöhnlich gut.

2 _____ Wind ist sehr stark.

3 _____ Temperaturen sind nicht typisch.

4 Bei _____ Sonne wird man schnell braun.

5 Aus _____ Grund ist das Klima hier besser als im Gebirge.

6.5 *Indefinite determiners*

The following words are also used with nouns and have identical endings to *dieser*.

jeder (used in singular)	each/every
jener (not used much in modern German. Use dieser . . . da for English 'that')	that
mancher (used in singular and plural)	many/many a/some
solcher (used in singular and plural)	such/such a
welcher? (used in singular and plural)	which?
alle	all (plural)
beide	both (plural)
einige	some (plural)
sämtliche	all, the entire (plural)

EXERCISE

E Insert the correct form of the indefinite determiners.

I _____ Gruppen sind aus Hamburg. (both)

2 Wir arbeiten mit _____ Gruppen zusammen. (both)

3 _____ ethnische Gruppe ist anders. (each)

4   _____ Vorteile hat das Leben in einer Großstadt? (which?)

5   _____ Leute wohnen lieber auf dem Lande. (some)

DERSELBE

Derselbe means 'the same/the same one'. Both the 'der' and the 'selbe' are declined. The forms are as follows.

	M	F	N	PI
Nom.	derselbe	dieselbe	dasselbe	dieselben
Acc.	denselben	dieselbe	dasselbe	dieselben
Dat.	demselben	derselben	demselben	denselben
Gen.	desselben	derselben	desselben	derselben

DERJENIGE

Derjenige means 'anyone (who)' or 'the person (who)'. It is usually followed by a relative pronoun. It is not very common, but you need to be able to recognize it.

	M	F	N	PI
Nom.	derjenige	diejenige	dasjenige	diejenigen
Acc.	denjenigen	diejenige	dasjenige	diejenigen
Dat.	demjenigen	derjenigen	demjenigen	denjenigen
Gen.	desjenigen	derjenigen	desjenigen	derjenigen

Example	Meaning
Diejenigen, die keine Stellen haben, können sich hier bewerben.	Those who have no job can apply here.
Mit _denjenigen_, die auf Urlaub sind, habe ich gestern gesprochen.	I spoke yesterday to those who are on holiday.
Für _diejenigen_, die dort arbeiten, macht das Oktoberfest nicht so viel Spaß.	For those who are working there the October Beer Festival is not so much fun.

EXERCISE

F   Translate these sentences into English.

   I   Er ist derselbe, der gestern im Konzert spielte.

   2   Diejenige, die Lust hat, Tennis zu spielen, kann jetzt gehen.

   3   Derjenige, der gerne Golf spielt, findet hier wunderbare Golfplätze.

   4   Für diejenigen, die gerne schwimmen, gibt es ein Freibad.

7

Pronouns

Contents

Pronouns stand instead of a noun. They are linked in gender and number to the noun to which they relate.

7.1 *Personal pronouns*

In correspondence *du* and *ihr* and all their forms (and possessive adjectives *dein* and *euer*) are written with capital letters. The Genitive is rarely used, so it is omitted here.

	Nom.	Acc.	Dat.
I	ich	mich	mir
you (sing. informal)	du	dich	dir
he	er	ihn	ihm
she	sie	sie	ihr
it	es	es	ihm
one	man	einen	einem

	Nom.	Acc.	Dat.
we	wir	uns	uns
you (formal)	Sie	Sie	Ihnen
you (pl. informal)	ihr	euch	euch
they	sie	sie	ihnen

PERSONAL PRONOUNS: GETTING TO KNOW 'YOU'

The English 'you' can be conveyed in a number of ways in German.

du	you – singular, informal; used when talking to children under 16, relatives, animals, close friends and people with left-wing/alternative leanings
man	one – much more common than 'one' in English; often translated as 'you', meaning 'people in general' – *man kann es verstehen* = you can understand it
Sie	you – singular or plural, formal; polite; used when addressing officials; used both for one person and many people
ihr	you – plural, informal; used when talking to more than one person informally (i.e. most or all of the group would be addressed individually as *du*)

EXERCISE

A Insert the correct personal pronoun in each sentence.

1 _____ nimmst 3 Zwiebeln. (you)

2 _____ nehme 250g Tomaten. (I)

3 _____ backen eine Pizza. (we)

4 _____ muss die Pizza 25 Minuten backen. (one)

5 Meine Brüder kommen uns besuchen. _____ essen sehr gerne Pizza. (they)

6 Meine Mutter macht sie oft für _____. (us)

7 Ich helfe _____ manchmal. (her)

8 Vater hilft ungern. Ich sehe _____ ganz selten in der Küche. (him)

7.2 *Reflexive pronouns*

	Acc.	Dat.
myself	mich	mir
yourself	dich	dir

	Acc.	Dat.
herself/himself/itself/oneself	sich	sich
ourselves	uns	uns
yourselves (formal)	sich	sich
yourselves (pl. informal)	euch	euch
themselves	sich	sich

Reflexive pronouns relate/reflect back to the subject of the verb. Usually they are used in the Accusative case, but there are exceptions.

Rule	Example	Meaning
Use Acc. for Direct Object	ich wasche mich	I wash myself
Use Dative where there is a Direct Object as well	ich wasche mir die Haare	I wash my hair (lit. the hair for myself)

EXERCISE

B   Insert the correct form of the reflexive pronoun in each sentence.

I   Ich wasche _____ die Haare.

2   Er wäscht _____.

3   Du erinnerst _____.

4   Wir setzen _____ hier hin.

5   Sie interessieren _____ für Kunst.

REFLEXIVE PRONOUNS AND REFLEXIVE VERBS

There are only ten commonly used 'true' reflexive verbs. These always *have* to be used reflexively. (See Chapter 10.)

Reflexive verb	Meaning	Example
sich bedanken (+ bei)	to thank sb	Ich habe mich bei dem Manager bedankt.
sich beeilen	to make haste	Wir haben uns beeilt.
sich befinden	to be situated, find oneself	Neuburg befindet sich an der Donau.
sich benehmen	to behave	Das Mädchen benimmt sich gut.

Reflexive verb	Meaning	Example
sich entschließen	to decide	Ich habe mich entschlossen, die Stelle zu nehmen.
sich erholen	to recover	Ich habe mich nach dem Stress erholt.
sich erkälten	to catch a cold	Sie hat sich in Leipzig erkältet.
sich verabschieden	to take one's leave	Sie haben sich von den Besuchern verabschiedet.
sich weigern	to refuse	Er hat sich geweigert, Militärdienst zu leisten.

EXERCISE

C Translate the following sentences into German.

1   The hotel is in Rostock.

2   My brother caught a cold there.

3   Now he has recovered.

4   He decided to go to Magdeburg.

5   We said goodbye to him.

7.3 *Relative pronouns*

	M	F	N	Pl
Nom.	der	die	das	die
Acc.	den	die	das	die
Dat.	dem	der	dem	**denen**
Gen.	**dessen**	**deren**	**dessen**	**deren**

In form, the relative pronoun is the **same as the definite article apart from** all the **Genitive** forms and the **Dative Plural**.

Relative pronouns relate back to a noun which has just been mentioned. They help you to put over information more concisely. Look at these pairs of sentences.

1   She is the woman. She works in the supermarket.

2   How much is the car? I saw the car last week.

3   Here is the man. I was speaking with the man.

4   Where is the woman? The woman's car was stolen.

It is possible to combine these sentences. In English, you can sometimes omit the relative pronoun, but in German it always has to be included.

English	German	Relative pronoun
She's the woman who works in the supermarket	Sie ist die Frau, **die** im Supermarkt arbeitet.	**die** – Fem. Sing. Nom. – subject of clause
How much is the car (which) I saw last week?	Was kostet das Auto, **das** ich letzte Woche sah?	**das** – Neut. Sing. Acc .– object of verb *sehen*
Here is the man I was speaking with.	Hier ist der Mann, mit **dem** ich sprach.	**dem** – Masc. Sing. Dat. after *mit*
Where is the woman whose car was stolen?	Wo ist die Frau, **deren** Auto gestohlen wurde?	**deren** – Fem. Sing. Gen. (the car *of* the woman)

Using the correct relative pronoun is easy in German if you work systematically.

1   First insert the **relative pronoun** into the English if it's not already there.

2   The **antecedent noun** (noun before the relative pronoun) determines the **number** and **gender** of the relative pronoun.

3   The **case** is determined by the **role** the relative pronoun plays in its own **clause.**

NB There is always a comma before the relative pronoun, and the relative pronoun sends the main verb to the end of the clause.

EXERCISES

D   Insert the correct form of the relative pronoun.

I   She is the woman **who** (Fem. Sing. Nom.) works in Berlin.

2   She is the woman **whose** (Fem. Sing. Gen.) firm is successful.

3   Here is the man (Masc. Sing. Dat.) I work with.

4   They are the people **whose** (Plural Gen) computers are new.

E   Now tackle the following sentences using the same method.

I   Where is the book I bought?

2   I saw the computer you bought.

3   That's the firm whose products are so good.

4   That's the building we work in.

5   Have you seen the machine we made?

6   I like the products you described.

7   Where are the managers whose products were so bad?

8   He is the man whose firm is in Berlin.

9   She is the woman I sold the books to.

10   That's the product I like.

7.4 *Interrogative pronouns*

In German the question 'who' or 'what' has different forms. The case is determined by the pronoun's role in its clause. Prepositions come before the interrogative pronoun, e.g. **Für wen** haben Sie es gekauft? **Mit wem** sind Sie in die Stadt gegangen?

		Who . . .?	What . . .?
Nom.	who/what	Wer?	Was . . .?
Acc.	whom/what	Wen . . .?	Was . . .?
Dat.	whom	Wem . . .?	
Gen.	whose	Wessen . . .?	

EXERCISE

F   How do you ask these questions in German?

1   Who is the manager?

2   Who did you see?

3   Whose products did you buy?

4   Who did you reserve it for?

5   Who did you go with?

6   Whose factory is that?

7   What is that?

8   Who did you help?

QUESTION WORDS INVOLVING PREPOSITIONS

In English we use two or more words to ask questions like 'For what purpose?' or 'What with?'. In German prepositions can be combined with '*wo*', or '*wor*' if they begin with a vowel, to make one composite word. They are very common, particularly since there are many verbs which are followed by prepositions. (See Chapter 10.)

Question word	Example	Meaning
wofür	Wofür interessieren Sie sich?	What are you interested in?
womit	Womit haben Sie das kombiniert?	What did you combine it with?
worauf	Worauf warten Sie?	What are you waiting for?
woraus	Woraus besteht das Produkt?	What does the product consist of?
worin	Worin sehen Sie die Gefahr?	Where do you see the danger in that?
worüber	Worüber sprechen die Politiker?	What are the politicians talking about?
wovon	Wovon hat sie gelebt?	What did she live off?
wozu	Wozu sollen wir warten?	What is the point of us waiting? (lit. 'to what end')

All these forms may be used in direct speech or indirect speech. In indirect speech the main verb is sent to the end of the clause:

Direct speech   Wofür interessieren Sie sich im Moment?

Indirect speech   Ich weiß nicht, wofür Sie sich im Moment interessieren.

The interrogative pronoun *welcher*, meaning 'which one', is not used very often. It is never used in the Genitive.)

	M	F	N	Pl
Nom.	welcher	welche	welches	welche
Acc.	welchen	welche	welches	welche
Dat.	welchem	welcher	welchem	welchen

EXERCISE

G   Translate the following sentences into German.

1   What is she interested in?

2   What is the firm waiting for?

3   Where do you see the problem?

4   What are you talking about?

5   I don't know what she is waiting for.

6   I know what they are interested in.

7.5 *Possessive pronouns*

These correspond to the words 'mine', 'hers', 'his', 'ours', 'yours', 'theirs'.

meiner, deiner, seiner, ihrer, unsrer, Ihrer, eurer, ihrer are all declined the same.

	M	F	N	Pl
Nom.	meiner	meine	meins	meine
Acc.	meinen	meine	meins	meine
Dat.	meinem	meiner	meinem	meiner
Gen.	meines	meiner	meines	meiner

English	German
Is that your umbrella? No it's his.	Ist das Ihr Regenschirm? Nein, es ist seiner.
Have you seen mine?	Haben Sie meinen gesehen?
No. He went with yours.	Nein, er ist mit Ihrem gegangen.

You may also find *der meinige, der deinige, der seinige, der ihrige, der unsrige, der Ihrige, der eurige, der ihrige* used for emphasis to mean 'mine', 'yours', etc., but these are fairly uncommon forms.

EXERCISE

H   Complete these examples in German with the correct form of the possessive pronoun.

  I   Das ist nicht mein Problem. Es ist _____. (deiner)

  2   Haben Sie Ihre Karte? Ich habe _____. (meiner)

  3   Ich habe meine Probleme diskutiert. Sie diskutierte _____. (ihrer)

  4   Ich machte es trotz meiner Probleme. Sie machte es trotz _____. (ihrer)

  5   Ich kaufe eine Kassette für meine Mutter. Du kaufst eine Kassette für _____. (deiner)

  6   Er nahm sein Auto. Ich nahm _____. (meiner)

  7   Das erste Konzert ist in meiner Stadt. Das zweite Konzert ist in _____. (ihrer)

  8   Wo sind die Büros? _____ ist im ersten Stock. (meiner)

  9   Ich sah meine Freundin. Paul sah _____. (seiner)

  10 Wir kauften unsere Fahrkarten. Sie kauften _____. (ihrer)

7.6 Demonstrative pronouns

	M	F	N	Pl
Nom.	dieser	diese	dies/dieses	diese
Acc.	diesen	diese	dieses	diese
Dat.	diesem	dieser	diesem	diesen
Gen.	dieses	dieser	dieses	dieser

NB The Nom. Neuter *dies* is more common than *dieses*.

Dieser can be used in place of a noun, to mean 'this one' or 'the latter'.

Welcher (which one) and *jener* (that one, the former) are declined like *dieser*.

Derjenige means 'the one (who)' or 'whoever' and is almost always followed by the relative pronoun. It is useful to recognize this form, but it is not so common in every-day speech. (See Chapter 6.)

The pronoun *wer* means 'anyone who' or 'whoever' or 'he/she/the person who' and is used to make generalizations.

Example	Meaning
Dieser ist interessant, jener ist langweilig.	The latter is interesting, the former is boring.
Ich weiß nicht, welcher am interessantesten ist.	I don't know which one is most interesting.
Derjenige, der das schmutzig gemacht hat, muss es sauber machen.	Whoever has made it dirty has to clean it up.
Wer nach Italien fahren will, muss viel Geld sparen.	Anyone who wants to go to Italy has to save a lot of money.

7.7 Indefinite pronouns

It may help to divide the indefinite pronouns into those followed by a singular and those followed by a plural verb.

Pronoun + singular verb	Example	Meaning
alles	Alles ist in Ordnung.	Everything is in order.
ein bisschen	Ein bisschen ist geblieben.	A little bit is left.
etwas	Etwas ist sehr komisch.	Something is very strange.
irgend etwas	Irgend etwas muss gemacht werden.	Something or other has to be done.
nichts	Nichts bleibt von der Innenstadt.	Nothing is left of the city centre.

Pronoun + singular verb	Example	Meaning
niemand	Niemand kann es erklären.	Nobody can explain it.
viel	Viel bleibt unausgesprochen.	A lot remains unsaid.
wenig	Wenig ist geplant worden.	Little has been planned.

EXERCISE

I Translate the following sentences into German.

1 Nobody understands it.

2 Everything is clear.

3 Something is broken.

4 Nothing is here.

5 A little bit is left.

Pronoun + plural verb	Example	Meaning
beide	Beide haben Schwierigkeiten.	Both have difficulties.
einige	Einige fahren auf Urlaub.	Some go on holiday.
ein paar	Ein paar fallen durch das Netz.	A few fall through the net.
manche	Manche haben keine Wohnung.	Some people (a fair number) have no flat.
mehrere	Mehrere haben nicht genug Geld.	Several do not have enough money.

EXERCISE

J Translate the following sentences into German.

1 Both have a lot of money.

2 A few had no flat.

3 Several had problems.

4 Some people had difficulties with flats.

8 Adjectives and adverbs

Contents

8.1 Using adjectives and adverbs

One form in the dictionary represents both adjective and adverb: *schnell* can mean 'quick' or 'quickly'. Adverbs never have extra endings. Adjectives always have endings except in the following cases.

ADJECTIVES WITH NO ENDINGS

Rule	Example	Exception
Adjective used after verbs	es ist *kalt*	
Adjective used adverbially before an adjective	es ist *wirklich* kalt	

Rule	Example	Exception
-er adjective of time – 1950s -er adjective – town names	in den *fünfziger* Jahren die *fünfziger* Jahre der *Frankfurter* Bahnhof die *Frankfurter* Messe	
halb and *ganz* used before geographical names	*halb* Berlin *ganz* Rostock	*halb* and *ganz* used before geographical names with an article der *halbe* Schwarzwald die *ganze* BRD
Certain colour adjectives	beige, crème, lila, oliv, orange, rosa e.g. ein *rosa* Kleid	-*farben* may be added, and this adjective has endings e.g. ein *rosafarbenes* Kleid
Adjectives in a very tiny number of set phrases	*Kölnisch* Wasser (Eau de Cologne)	

EXERCISE

A   Insert the correct form of the adjective in each sentence.

1   Die _____ Messe hat eine lange Tradition. (Leipzig)

2   _____ Deutschland litt unter den Folgen des Krieges. (ganz)

3   In den _____ Jahren protestierten viele DDR-Bürger gegen das Regime. (achtziger)

4   Es war _____ warm in Halle. (wirklich)

5   Die _____ Ostseeküste ist sehr beliebt bei Touristen. (ganz)

6   Vom Standpunkt der Literaturgeschichte ist Weimar besonders _____. (interessant)

8.2 *Adjective endings*

There are three types of adjective endings, weak, mixed and strong. Their use is shown after the forms. The bold endings may help you learn the tables more easily.

Weak endings	M	F	N	Pl
Nom.	e	e	e	en
Acc.	en	e	e	en
Dat.	en	en	en	en
Gen.	en	en	en	en

Mixed endings	M	F	N	Pl
Nom.	**er**	e	**es**	en
Acc.	en	e	**es**	en
Dat.	en	en	en	en
Gen.	en	en	en	en

Strong endings	M	F	N	Pl
Nom.	**er**	e	**es**	e
Acc.	en	e	**es**	e
Dat.	em	er	em	en
Gen.	en	er	en	er

ADJECTIVE ENDINGS: USE

Weak	Mixed	Strong
After definite article Das *neue* Museum ist am Rhein.	After *ein* and *kein* Ein *neues* Museum öffnet bald.	When there is no determiner *Neue* Museen sind immer interessant.
After *dieser, welcher, jener, jeder* Dieser *neue* Konferenzraum ist erstklassig.	After all possessive adjectives *mein, dein* etc Ihr *neuer* Konferenzraum ist hervorragend.	After numbers Zwei *moderne* Konferenz-räume sind im ersten Stock.
After *alle* Alle *modernen* Räume sind klimatisiert.		After indefinite determiners *viel, einige, mehrere, viele*, etc. viel *gutes* Bier Einige *neue* Räume

Weak endings are either -*e*, in the bold area, or -*en* outside it. Outside the bold area the Mixed endings are all -*en*. The Strong endings are identical to the endings of *dieser*, apart from the Genitive Singular Masc. and Neuter. Here the noun normally adds -*s*, so the Genitive is already visible, e.g. trotz *schlechten* Wetters.

A row of adjectives before a noun all have the same endings. Es war ein *schöner, warmer* Abend. (NB Possessive adjectives *mein*, etc. need to be learnt separately. See 8.5.)

EXERCISE

B Insert the correct form of the adjective.

I Sie fahren durch eine _____ Stadt. (klein)

2 Für _____ Touristen gibt es Prospekte auf Deutsch und Englisch. (englisch)

3 Jeder _____ Gast kann sich in das Gästebuch eintragen. (neu)

4 Mein _____ Reiseführer ist nicht mehr sehr nützlich. (alt)

5 Fünf _____ Hotels existieren nicht mehr. (zentral)

6 Einige _____ Sehenswürdigkeiten sind noch geöffnet. (historisch)

7 Es gibt _____ Restaurants in der Nähe des Marktplatzes. (vietnamesisch)

8 Sie haben den _____ Bahnhof restauriert. (alt)

8.3 *Irregular spellings of adjectives*

Rule	Adjective	Example
Adjectives in -*el* lose the last e when endings are added	dunkel flexibel, plausibel	eine *dunkle* Nacht ein *flexibles* Programm
Adjectives ending in -*er* lose the last e when endings are added	makaber, sauer, teuer	ein *saurer* Wein ein *teurer* Wagen
hoch loses the c when endings are added	hoch	ein *hoher* Berg

EXERCISE

C Insert the correct form of each adjective.

I Das ist ein _____ Produkt. (teuer)

2 Das ist eine _____ Lösung. (flexibel)

3 Das ist eine sehr _____ Inflationsrate. (hoch)

4 Leider ist das die _____ Wahrheit. (bitter)

8.4 *Comparative and superlative of adjectives and adverbs*

The comparative is used to compare two items. In English it is normally formed either by adding -*er* to the adj. (e.g. colder) or by using the word 'more' + adj. (e.g. more sensitive). In German *mehr* is only combined with nouns – *mehr Zeit* = more time;

*mehr Arbe*it = more work. ALL comparative adjectives in German are in the form of one single word. The superlative is used to compare three or more items.

Form	Rule	Example
Comparative adjectives	Add -*er* or umlaut + -*er* to adjective + ending if needed	Das ist ein *schnellerer* Zug.
Comparative adverbs	Add -*er* or umlaut + -*er* to adjective	Ein ICE fährt *schneller* als ein Eilzug.
Superlative adjectives	Add -*st/est* or umlaut + -*st/est* to adjective + ending if needed	Das ist der *schnellste* Zug.
Superlative adverbs	am + superlative adjective + -en	Der ICE fährt am schnellsten.

There are a number of exceptions, which are listed below.

IRREGULAR COMPARATIVES AND SUPERLATIVES (ADVERB FORM OF SUPERLATIVE GIVEN)

Rule	Adjective/Adverb	Comparative	Superlative
a > ä	alt	älter	am ältesten
	arm	ärmer	am ärmsten
	hart	härter	am härtesten
	kalt	kälter	am kältesten
	krank	kränker	am kränksten
	lang	länger	am längsten
	scharf	schärfer	am schärfsten
	schwach	schwächer	am schwächsten
	schwarz	schwärzer	am schwärzesten
	stark	stärker	am stärksten
	warm	wärmer	am wärmsten
u > ü	dumm	dümmer	am dümmsten
	jung	jünger	am jüngsten
	klug	klüger	am klügsten
	kurz	kürzer	am kürzesten
o > ö	grob	gröber	am gröbsten
	groß	größer	am größten
Adjectives ending in -*el* and -*en* and -*er* lose final e in comparative	flexibel	flexibler	am flexibelsten
	trocken	trockner	am trockensten
	teuer	teurer	am teuersten

Rule	Adjective/Adverb	Comparative	Superlative
Irregular forms	gut	besser	am besten
	hoch	höher	am höchsten
	nah	näher	am nächsten
	viel	mehr	am meisten

Comparisons are made as follows.

Rule	Adjective	Adverb
nicht so + adjective/adverb + *wie*	Die Temperatur ist nicht so hoch wie in Madrid.	Sie spielt nicht so gut wie ihre Schwester.
genauso + adjective + *wie*	Die Temperatur ist genauso hoch wie in Greifswald.	Sie spielt genauso gut wie ihre Kollegin.
X *ist* + comparative adjective/adverb + *als* Y	Kiel ist kälter als Frankfurt.	Sie spielt besser als ihr Chef.
'Coldest city *in* Europa': *in* is conveyed by the Genitive in German.	Das ist die kälteste Stadt Europas.	
'Most + adjective/adverb': 'most' can be conveyed by *außerordentlich/höchst* + adjective/adverb	Das ist ein außerordentlich interessanter Film.	Sie spielt außerordentlich langsam.

One or two comparative adjectives are not used in comparisons but convey the idea of 'fairly' + adjective.

Comparative adjective	Meaning	Example
älter	elderly	Er ist ein *älterer* Herr.
größer	largish	Das ist eine *größere* Gruppe.
kleiner	smallish	*kleinere* Geldsummen

EXERCISE

D Insert the correct words in the following sentences.

1 Im Norden ist es windiger _____ im Süden. (than)

2 In Erfurt ist es genauso warm _____ in Magdeburg. (as)

3 In Kiel ist es am _____. (coldest)

4 München ist mit 20 Grad die _____ Stadt Deutschlands. (warmest)

5   Gestern war es im Südwesten _____ sonnig. (longer)

6   Im Osten wird der Wind am _____ sein. (weakest)

7   In Nürnberg war die Temperatur _____ als in Erfurt. (higher)

8   In Saarbrücken hat es gestern am _____ geregnet. (most)

8.5 *Possessive adjectives*

These correspond to the adjectives 'my', 'your', etc. in English. *Dein, sein, ihr* (her), *unser, Ihr, euer* and *ihr* (their) are all declined the same as *mein* and the negative indefinite article *kein*. They are followed by Mixed adjective endings.

	M	F	N	Pl
Nom.	mein	meine	mein	meine
Acc.	meinen	meine	mein	meine
Dat.	meinem	meiner	meinem	meinen
Gen.	meines	meiner	meines	meiner

EXERCISE

E   Translate the following sentences into English.

1   This is my grammar school.

2   Frau Nause is my new teacher.

3   I am working with Anna, my classmate.

4   Her favourite subject is art.

5   Our next exams are in July.

8.6 *The determiners* dieser *(this),* jener *(that),* jeder *(each/every) and* welcher? *(which?)*

All are declined the same as *dieser* and are followed by weak adjective endings.

	M	F	N	Pl
Nom.	dieser	diese	dieses	diese
Acc.	diesen	diese	dieses	diese
Dat.	diesem	dieser	diesem	diesen
Gen.	dieses	dieser	dieses	dieser

EXERCISE

F   Insert the correct form of the determiner.

1   _____ Region ist sehr flach. (this)

2   _____ Fluss fließt durch Frankfurt? (which?)

3   Sind _____ Berge im Süden Deutschlands? (those)

4   In _____ Naturpark kann man wunderschön wandern. (every)

5   An _____ Küste liegt Bremerhaven? (which?)

8.7 *Adjectives with cases*

Certain adjectives are followed by a particular case. There are a few frequently used adjectives which are followed by the Accusative and quite a number followed by the Dative. It's rare to find any followed by the Genitive in modern German.

The Accusative ones are given first, then the Dative. Each group is in alphabetical order.

Adjective + Acc.	Adjective	Example	Meaning
Used in phrases with *sein* or *werden*	gewohnt sein	Ich bin es gewohnt.	I am used to it.
	los sein/werden	Ich bin es los.	I am rid of it.
	satt sein/werden	Ich werde es satt.	I am becoming fed up of it.

Adjective + Dat.	Adjective	Example	Meaning
	ähnlich	Sie sieht ihrer Schwester ähnlich.	She looks similar to her sister.
	behilflich	Sie war ihm behilflich.	She was helpful to him.
	bekannt	Das ist mir bekannt.	I am aware of that.
	böse	Bist du mir böse?	Are you cross with me?
	dankbar	Er war ihr dankbar.	He was grateful to her.
	egal/gleich	Das ist mir egal.	It's all the same to me.
	klar	Das ist mir klar.	That is clear to me.
	lästig	Das ist uns lästig.	That is a nuisance to us.
	nützlich	Es war uns nützlich.	It was useful to us.
	peinlich	Das ist mir peinlich.	That is embarrassing for me.
	schuldig	Was bin ich Ihnen schuldig?	What do I owe you?
	unbegreiflich	Das bleibt mir unbegreiflich.	That remains a mystery to me.

EXERCISE

G Insert the correct adjective in each sentence.

1   Ich bin es _____, im Zug schlecht zu essen. (fed up)

2   Es ist mir _____, ob es teuer ist. (all the same)

3   Es ist mir einfach _____, Reiseproviant mitzuschleppen. (a nuisance)

4   Eigentlich ist es mir _____, warum sie nichts Leckeres servieren. (incomprehensible/a mystery)

5   Den Kellnern muss es oft _____ sein, wenn das Essen so miserabel ist. (embarrassing)

6   Meiner Mutter bin ich _____, wenn sie mir ein Lunchpaket mitgibt. (grateful)

8.8 *Adjectives with prepositions*

A number of adjectives are followed by prepositions. Those marked with an asterisk (*) often have the adjective after the preposition + noun/pronoun. Those followed by the Accusative are listed first, then those followed by the Dative. Each group is listed alphabetically by preposition.

ADJECTIVES WITH PREPOSITIONS + ACCUSATIVE

Adjective	Preposition	Meaning	Example
angewiesen*	auf	reliant on	Er ist auf ihn angewiesen.
böse	auf	angry with	Sie ist böse auf ihn.
eifersüchtig	auf	jealous of	Sie ist eifersüchtig auf ihre Schwester.
neidisch	auf	envious of	Er ist neidisch auf seinen Freund.
scharf	auf	keen on	Sie ist scharf auf die Rockgruppe.
stolz	auf	proud of	Wir sind stolz auf unsere Produkte.
vorbereitet*	auf	prepared for	Ich bin auf die Prüfung vorbereitet.
wütend	auf	furious with	Er war wütend auf ihn.
dankbar	für	grateful for	Wir sind dankbar für Ihre Hilfe.

Adjective	Preposition	Meaning	Example
empfänglich	für	receptive to	Sie sind empfänglich für neue Ideen.
geeignet	für	suitable for	Das ist geeignet für eine kleine Gruppe.
typisch	für	typical of	Das ist typisch für meine Region.
zuständig*	für	responsible for	Ich bin für Kunden zuständig.
allergisch	gegen	allergic to	Sie ist allergisch gegen Katzen.
verliebt*	in	in love with	Er ist in sie verliebt.

ADJECTIVES WITH PREPOSITIONS + DATIVE

Adjective	Preposition	Meaning	Example
arm/reich	an	low/high in	Es ist arm/reich an Kalorien
interesssiert*	an	interested in	Ich bin an Politik interessiert.
gleichgültig	gegenüber (follows noun/pronoun)	indifferent to	Ihm gegenüber ist sie gleichgültig.
einverstanden*	mit	in agreement with	Wir sind mit ihnen einverstanden.
verheiratet	mit	married to	Sie ist mit ihm verheiratet.
abhängig/ unabhängig	von	dependent on/ independent of	Sie ist unabhängig von uns.
begeistert	von	enthusiastic about	Ich bin begeistert von der Musik.
überzeugt	von	convinced of	Ich bin überzeugt von seiner Unschuld.
blass	vor	pale with	Sie war blass vor Angst.
rot	vor	red with	Er war rot vor Wut.
berechtigt*	zu	entitled to	Sie sind zu einer Ermäßigung berechtigt.
bereit*	zu	ready for	Sie sind zu allem bereit.

EXERCISE

H Insert the correct preposition in each of the sentences.

  I Er ist vorbereitet _____ die Expansion der Firma.

  2 Der Preis ist unabhängig _____ der Inflationsrate.

  3 Das ist typisch _____ unsere Produkte.

  4 Der Marketing-Manager ist sehr empfänglich _____ neue Impulse.

  5 Die Praktikantin war sehr dankbar _____ die Hilfe.

  6 Sie sind _____ den Kunden einverstanden.

  7 Viele sind gleichgültig _____ den Innovationen.

  8 Sie sind überzeugt _____ der Richtigkeit der neuen Pläne.

  9 Die Abteilungsleiterin ist einverstanden _____ den Plänen.

 10 Sie ist _____ Werbung zuständig.

 11 Der Finanzmanager ist _____ Computern interessiert.

 12 Sie sind sehr stolz _____ die Exporte.

 13 Er ist begeistert _____ dem neuen Modell.

 14 Das Produkt ist reich _____ Kalorien.

 15 Das ist geeignet _____ das Ausland.

8.9 *Adverbs of time, place, attitude, reason and degree*

These adverbs are in very common usage. They are in five groups, with each group in alphabetical order. You can use one or several in a sentence. NB Watch word order with adverbs of time, manner and place. (See Chapter 3.)

ADVERBS OF TIME

bald (soon), früher (earlier), gestern (yesterday), häufig (frequently), heute (today), immer (always), jetzt (now), lange (for a long time), manchmal (sometimes), morgen (tomorrow), nachher (afterwards), neulich (recently), nie (never), selten (seldom), sofort (immediately), später (later), vorher (previously), wieder (again).

ADVERBS OF PLACE

dort (there), draußen (outside), hier (here), innen (inside), nirgendwo (nowhere), oben (at the top), überall (everywhere), unten (at the bottom).

ADVERBS OF ATTITUDE

bestimmt (definitely), glücklicherweise (luckily), hoffentlich (hopefully), komischerweise (funnily enough), leider (unfortunately), natürlich/selbstverständlich (naturally), normalerweise (normally), vielleicht (perhaps), wahrscheinlich (probably).

ADVERBS OF REASON

dennoch/trotzdem (nevertheless), deshalb/deswegen (therefore), sonst (otherwise).

ADVERBS OF DEGREE

außerordentlich (exceptionally), besonders (especially), etwas (somewhat), fast (almost), ganz (completely), kaum (scarcely), relativ (relatively), sehr (very), vollkommen (completely), ziemlich (fairly), zu (too).

EXERCISE

I   Insert the correct adverb in each sentence.

1   _____ gibt es viele karitative Organisationen in Deutschland. (today)

2   _____ gibt es interessante lokale Projekte. (everywhere)

3   _____ versuchen einige Gruppen, auch international aktiv zu sein. (naturally)

4   Sie helfen _____, wo sie gebraucht werden. (there/in the place)

5   Sie freuen sich _____, Spenden zu bekommen. (always)

6   _____ haben sie nicht immer genug Geld, um viel machen zu können. (sometimes)

7   Sie kooperieren _____ mit internationalen Organisationen. (nevertheless)

8   _____ fühlen sie sich manchmal sehr isoliert. (otherwise)

8.10 *Interrogative adverbs*

Interrogative adverb	Meaning	Example
wann?	When?	Wann ist sie zu Hause?
warum?	Why?	Warum arbeiten Sie hier?
wie lange?	How long?	Wie lange bleiben Sie?
wie?	How?	Wie kommen Sie hierher?

Interrogative adverb	Meaning	Example
wieso?	How come?	Wieso bleiben Sie so lange?
wo?	Where?	Wo wohnen Sie?
woher?	Where from?	Woher kommen Sie?
wohin?	Where to?	Wohin fliegen Sie?
wozu?	For what purpose?	Wozu brauche ich das?

EXERCISE

J   Translate the following questions into German.

1   When are you going to Germany?

2   How long are you staying there?

3   Where are you living at the moment?

4   Why are you working in Bremen?

5   Where are you going at Christmas?

Prepositions

Contents

Prepositions may indicate the position of one thing with relation to another. They may also show the relationship between two nouns/pronouns.

It is very common for the preposition used in German to be different from its English equivalent. The English take medicine 'for' a cold. The Germans take medicine 'against' a cold. The English congratulate people 'on' their birthday. The Germans congratulate them 'to' their birthday. For this reason it is important to realize that most German prepositions have several possible translations in English, and vice versa.

9.1 *Prepositions with the Accusative*

It may help to remember the prepositions with Accusative if you think of the first letter of each preposition – *durch, ohne, gegen, wider, um, für* = DOGWUF! The prepositions *entlang, per* and *pro* also take the Accusative.

Preposition	Meaning	Example
durch	through	Sie ging durch den Park.
ohne	without	Ich machte es ohne meine Mutter.

Preposition	Meaning	Example
gegen	against	Sie spielten gegen die Dänen.
	in exchange for	Ich tauschte das gegen ein anderes Modell um.
	for (as an antidote)	Tabletten gegen Husten
	getting on for (time)	gegen Mittag
wider	against (someone's will)	Das war wider meinen Willen
um	round	Sie liefen um den Block.
	at (time)	um Viertel nach eins
für	for	Es war ein Geschenk für die Gruppe.
entlang (usually after the noun)	along	Sie ging die Straße entlang.
per	by (means of)	Sie schicken es per Fax/Post.
pro	per	Das Zimmer kostet DM200 pro Nacht.

PREPOSITIONS WITH ACCUSATIVE: SET PHRASES

durch Zufall	by chance
Die Preise sind *um* 5 Prozent gestiegen.	The prices went up by 5 per cent.
Ich verlängerte meinen Urlaub *um* eine Woche	I extended my holiday by a week.

EXERCISE

A   Insert the most appropriate preposition in each sentence.

1   Ich kaufte es _____ meine Mutter.

2   Sie machte es _____ meinen Willen.

3   Sie ging _____ den Wald, weil es da so schön war.

4   Sie joggte dann viermal _____ den Block.

5   _____ einen Regenschirm werden Sie nass werden.

6   Sie nehmen Tabletten _____ Kopfschmerzen.

7   Ich fuhr mit meiner Familie den Rhein _____.

8   Meine Oma bezahlte viel _____ Quadratmeter für ihre Wohnung.

9   Mein Mann und ich spielten _____ meine Schwiegereltern.

10   Er schickte eine Geburtstagskarte _____ e-mail.

EXPRESSING THE ENGLISH 'FOR' IN GERMAN

Rule	Example
für is used for presents/gifts	Ich kaufte es für meine Schwester. (for my sister)
für is occasionally used for future events	Ich fahre für zwei Wochen zur Ostsee. (for two weeks)
Dative is often used for getting sth for sb	Ich kaufte es ihr. (for her)
gegen + illnesses/complaints	Tabletten gegen Halsschmerzen (for a sore throat)
seit + time phrases in the past	Ich wohne hier seit vier Jahren. (for four years)
zu + occasions	Ich bekam es zum Geburtstag. (for my birthday) Sie schenkte das zu Weihnachten. (for Christmas)
prepositions + certain verbs (See Chapter 10.)	Ich warte auf meinen Chef. (wait for) Ich sehne mich nach Wärme. (long for) Ich suche nach einer Stelle. (look for) Er bewirbt sich um ein Stipendium. (apply for) Ich bitte dich um Hilfe. (ask for) Ich kämpfe um mein Leben. (fight for)

EXERCISE

B   Insert the correct word for 'for' in each sentence.

1   He is looking for his umbrella. Er sucht _____ seinem Regenschirm.

2   I am longing for the sun. Ich sehne mich _____ der Sonne.

3   The cream is for sunburn. Die Salbe ist _____ Sonnenbrand.

4   We got gloves for Christmas. Wir bekamen Handschuhe _____ Weihnachten.

5   We are going to the North Pole for three months. Wir fahren _____ drei Monate zum Nordpol.

6   He has been living for two months in the rainforest. Er wohnt _____ zwei Monaten im Regenwald.

9.2 *Prepositions with the Dative*

This 'rhyme' may help you to remember the Prepositions with Dative:

'Dative preps are but a few – *aus, bei, mit, nach, seit, von, zu,* and *gegenüber,* too.'

Außer (except) also takes the Dative.

Preposition	Meaning	Example
aus	out of	Er kam aus der Boutique.
	from (origins)	Sie kommt aus Schottland.
	made of	Es ist aus Plastik.
	dating from	Das ist aus dem 20. Jahrhundert.
	for (a reason)	Aus diesem Grund ist es gut.
bei	at the house/shop of sb	Wir wohnten bei meinem Onkel.
	at (firm/workplace)	Sie arbeitet bei Siemens
	on the occasion of	bei gutem Wetter
	with (on one's person)	Ich habe meinen Pass bei mir.
mit	with	Ich fuhr mit meinem Bruder.
	by (transport)	Er fährt mit der Bahn.
nach	after	Das war nach dem Mittagessen.
	to (countries/cities)	Wir fahren nach Celle.
	according to (*nach* after noun)	meiner Meinung nach
	in the style of	nach englischer Art
seit	since	Sie ist seit 1998 hier.
	for (past time)	Sie leben seit vier Jahren hier. (See Chapter 10.)
von	from/of	Ich kaufte es vom Autohändler.
zu	to places, buildings	Sie gehen zur Bushaltestelle.
	at (prices)	ein T-Shirt zu DM10
gegenüber	opposite (before or after noun)	Es ist gegenüber dem Schloss.
	in relation to (after noun/pronoun)	Mir gegenüber ist er nett.
außer	except	Außer ihm waren sie nett.

EXERCISE

C Insert the most appropriate Dative preposition in each sentence.

1 Sie ist _____ ihrer Schwester nach Polen gefahren.

2 Sie ist Engländerin, aber er kommt _____ Schottland.

3 Er lebt _____ drei Jahren in den USA.

4 Das Reisebüro ist _____ dem Bahnhof.

5 Sie haben ihre Koffer _____ C & A gekauft.

6 _____ dem Urlaub in Spanien ist es schwer, wieder ins Büro zu gehen.

7 Bern ist die Hauptstadt _____ der Schweiz.

8   Weil er so oft auf Geschäftsreisen ist, ist er nicht oft _____ Hause.

9   Wir flogen _____ Düsseldorf nach Wien.

10   Sie arbeitete zehn Jahre _____ Mercedes.

PREPOSITIONS WITH THE DATIVE: SET PHRASES

Phrase	Meaning
außer Atem sein	to be out of breath
außer Betrieb	out of order/not working
außer Gefahr	out of danger
bei der Arbeit	at work
mit der Zeit	in the course of time
mit fünfzig	at the age of 50
von mir *aus*	as far as I am concerned
von Beruf her	by profession
zu Fuß	on foot
zu Hause	at home
zum Beispiel	for example
zum Geburtstag	for (somebody's) birthday
zur Not	at a pinch
zur Sache kommen	to get to the point

9.3 *Prepositions with the Accusative or Dative*

The following prepositions take either the Dative or the Accusative.

Case	Rule	Example
Accusative	movement *into* a place.	Wir gehen in die Stadt.
Dative	position *in* a place movement *within* a place	Sie wohnt in der Stadt. Sie wandert im Gebirge.

Preposition	Meaning	Accusative example	Dative example
an	to/at/on	Sie fuhr an die Küste.	Er war am Bahnhof.
auf	onto/on to/at	Es fiel auf den Tisch. Sie geht auf eine Tagung.	Es war auf dem Tisch. Das war auf einer Tagung.
hinter	behind	Er ging hinter das Café.	Es war hinter dem Café.

Preposition	Meaning	Accusative example	Dative example
in	into/in on (floor of a building)	Sie fuhr in die Stadtmitte.	Das Theater ist in der Stadtmitte. Die Wohnung war im dritten Stock.
neben	next to	Sie setzte sich neben ihre Freundin.	Die Bank ist neben dem Dom.
über	above/over via	Ich ging über die Straße. Sie fuhr über die Schweiz.	Das Foto war über dem Schrank. –
unter	under	Ich ging unter die Brücke.	Das Dorf war unter der Schneegrenze.
vor	in front of/before ago	Sie ging vor das Rathaus. –	Die Statue ist vor dem Rathaus. Das war vor 3 Jahren.
zwischen	between	RARELY USED	Es ist zwischen dem Dom und der Post.

EXERCISE

D Insert the correct word for 'the'.

1 Ich war in _____ Stadtmitte.

2 Sie ging in _____ Bäckerei.

3 Wir spielten hinter _____ Supermarkt.

4 Der Weihnachtsmarkt war vor _____ Rathaus.

5 Das Museum ist zwischen dem Dom und _____ Bahnhof.

6 Sie ging in _____ Galerie.

7 Wir treffen uns in _____ Eisdiele.

SET PHRASES INVOLVING 'IN' AND 'UNTER' + DATIVE

Phrase	Meaning
im 2. Stock	on the 2nd floor
im Durchschnitt	on average
im Fernsehen/Radio	on television/the radio
unter anderem	among other things

Phrase	Meaning
unter diesen Umständen	in these circumstances
unter uns	between ourselves
unter vier Augen	in private

EXERCISE

E Translate the following sentences.

1 Among other things drugs are expensive.

2 Between ourselves I think she is ill.

3 The boxer lives on the first floor.

4 The programme on drugs was on television.

5 We spoke in private about her illness.

EXPRESSING 'TO' IN GERMAN (ROUGHLY IN ORDER OF FREQUENCY)

Rule	Example
nach + towns and countries	Ich fahre *nach* Polen.
in + fem and plural countries	Sie fährt *in* die Türkei.
in + going inside buildings	Sie geht *ins* Kino/Theater.
	Wir gehen *in* die Oper.
in meaning 'into' an area	Er fährt *in* den Böhmerwald.
zu + buildings and people's houses	Er fährt *zum* Bahnhof.
	Sie fährt *zu* ihrer Mutter.
auf + set phrases	Er fährt *aufs* Land.
	Sie geht *auf* die Toilette.
an + set phrases	Sie fahren *ans* Meer.

Certain prepositions can be combined with forms of the definite article to make shorter forms. The most common examples are listed below.

Preposition	Short form Accusative	Short form Dative
an	ans	am
bei		beim
für	fürs	

Preposition	Short form Accusative	Short form Dative
in	ins	im
von		vom
zu		zum (Masc./Neut.) zur (Fem.)

EXERCISES

F Insert the correct preposition (+ definite article if needed) for 'to' in each sentence.

1 Sie fliegt _____ Dresden.

2 Sie geht _____ Bahnhof.

3 Ich fahre _____ Stadt.

4 Wir fahren _____ meinem Bruder.

5 Meine Schwester fährt _____ Meer.

6 Ich gehe heute _____ Kino.

7 Er geht _____ die Toilette.

8 Sie fliegt _____ die USA.

G Now translate the following sentences.

1 The supermarket is in the town centre.

2 He goes into the department store.

3 They are in the gallery.

4 He went into the cinema.

5 It is between the chemist's and the café.

9.4 *Prepositions with the Genitive*

Preposition	Meaning	Example
während	during	Während des Krieges war alles schwer.
wegen	because of	Wegen des Regens konnten sie nicht spielen.
statt	instead of	Ich kaufte einen Pulli statt einer Jacke.
trotz	in spite of	Sie arbeiteten trotz des Streiks.

A NUMBER OF PREPOSITIONS MAY BE USED WITH THE GENITIVE OR FOLLOWED BY *VON*

Preposition	Meaning	Examples
außerhalb/innerhalb	outside/inside	Der Campingplatz ist außerhalb der Stadt. Der Campingplatz ist innerhalb von der Stadt.
oberhalb/unterhalb	above/below	Die Burg ist oberhalb des Dorfes. Die Burg ist unterhalb vom Dorf.

In formal German there are a number of other prepositions you may see written:

Preposition	Meaning	Example
angesichts	in view of	angesichts der Inflationsrate
diesseits	on this side of	Diesseits der Grenze gibt es keine Probleme.
jenseits	on the other side of	jenseits der Grenze

EXERCISE

H Insert the most appropriate preposition in each sentence.

1. _____ des schlechten Wetters gingen sie schwimmen.

2. _____ der Mittagspause haben sie eingekauft.

3. _____ des Schnees war es nicht möglich, nach Italien zu fahren.

4. _____ der Schneegrenze konnte man eine Wanderung machen.

5. _____ der Schneegrenze konnte man Ski fahren.

You may find it helpful to underline all the prepositions in a short article in German. Which are most common? Repeat the exercise with another article and compare your findings.

10

Verbs

Contents

10.1 *Introduction*

This chapter deals with verbs, their forms and their uses. You can read it from beginning to end or dip in and out. Where appropriate, information is repeated (e.g. the Present tense of *haben* and *sein* appears under both Present tense and Perfect tense. The section on Conditional sentences includes material on the Subjunctive mood.) Do use the Index! Don't be afraid to look up more than one section!

For each section, verbs are dealt with in this order:

- Weak verbs
- Strong verbs
- Mixed verbs
- *haben* and *sein*
- *werden* and *lassen*
- Modal verbs

All infinitives except *sein* (to be) and *tun* (to do) end in *-en*, *-eln* or *-ern*. The infinitive is the main form of the verb which is listed in the dictionary.

EXERCISE

A Look at each word. Is it an infinitive or not?

I	expandieren
2	tun
3	immun
4	investieren
5	innovativ
6	handeln
7	sein
8	verkaufen

FORMING THE STEM OF A VERB

Rule	Infinitive	Stem
-en verbs lose the *en*	spielen	spiel
-eln verbs lose the *n*	sammeln	sammel
-ern verbs lose the *n*	wandern	wander

TRANSLATING TENSE FORMS INTO ENGLISH

In German each tense can be translated in English as the simple form (e.g. I buy) or the continuous form (e.g. I am buying).

German	English simple form	English continuous form
ich gehe	I go	I am going
er besuchte	he visited	he was visiting
wir gingen	we went	we were going
Sie haben studiert	you have studied	you have been studying (usually translated into German by Present tense + *seit* + time phrase)
sie hatten studiert	they had studied	they had been studying (usually translated into German by Imperfect tense + *seit* + time phrase)

10.2 *Weak, strong and mixed verbs,* haben, sein, werden, lassen *and modal verbs*

In German most verbs are **weak**. Weak verbs form the Imperfect and Perfect by adding elements to the stem, just as English weak verbs do: *park*, I *parked*, I have *parked*. Most can be easily recognized.

Some of the most frequently used verbs in the German language are **strong** verbs, e.g. *essen, finden, gehen*. Strong verbs show more noticeable vowel changes, like English strong verbs e.g. *I drink*, I *drank*, I *have drunk*. They are listed at the back of this book.

Mixed verbs – only nine are in common usage (see list below).

Weak infinitive endings	Example	Exception
-*eln*	handeln	
-*ern*	wandern	
-*ieren*	diskutieren	*frieren* and *verlieren* are strong verbs
-*tmen*	atmen	

NINE COMMONLY USED MIXED VERBS

Infinitive	Imperfect	Past participle
brennen	brannte	gebrannt
bringen	brachte	gebracht
denken	dachte	gedacht

Infinitive	Imperfect	Past participle
kennen	kannte	gekannt
nennen	nannte	genannt
rennen	rannte	gerannt
senden	sandte	gesandt
wenden	wandte	gewandt
wissen	wusste	gewusst

KEY FEATURES OF WEAK, STRONG AND MIXED VERBS

	Weak verbs	Strong verbs	Mixed verbs
Present tense	Stem vowel *never* changes	Stem vowel *may* change in *du* form + 3rd Pers. Sing.	Stem vowel *may* change in 1st Pers. Sing., *du* + 3rd Pers. Sing. forms
e.g.	ich parke, du parkst, er parkt	ich spreche, du sprichst, er spricht	ich weiß, du weißt, er weiß
Imperfect tense	Stem vowel *never* changes 1st/3rd Pers. Sing. ends in -te	Stem vowel *always* changes 1st/3rd Pers. Sing. ends in consonant	Stem vowel *always* changes 1st/3rd Pers. Sing. ends in –te
e.g.	er parkte	er sprach	er wusste
Past participle	ends in -t stem vowel *never* changes	ends in -n stem vowel *may* change	ends in -t stem vowel *always* changes
e.g.	geparkt	gesprochen	gewusst

EXERCISE

B   Are these verbs strong or weak?

1   ändern

2   essen

3   gehen

4   angeln

5   analysieren

6   adaptieren

7   trinken

8 verlieren

9 wandern

10 parken

Separable and inseparable verbs are formed in the same way as the basic forms, e.g. *zurückfaxen* like *faxen*, *aufessen* like *essen*, *verkaufen* like *kaufen*, etc.

HABEN, SEIN, WERDEN, LASSEN AND MODAL VERBS

Haben and *sein* are irregular. They are auxiliary verbs, used to form the Perfect, Pluperfect, Future Perfect and Conditional Perfect tenses.

Werden is used to form the Future tense and the Passive, as well as meaning 'to become'. *Lassen* means to 'let' or 'leave', but is also used with infinitives to mean 'to have something done'.

There are six Modal verbs – *dürfen* (to be allowed to), *können* (to be able to), *mögen* (to like to), *müssen* (to have to), *sollen* (to be supposed to) and *wollen* (to want to). They can be used on their own or with infinitives (see Word order and Chapter 1).

10.3 *Present tense*

	Example	Meaning
Describe actions happening now	Sie studiert Medizin.	She is studying medicine.
Describe things done on a regular basis	Montags spiele ich immer Badminton.	On Mondays I always play badminton.
Used with *seit* + Dat. time phrase for actions in the past which still continue	Wir lernen seit zwei Jahren Deutsch.	We have been learning German for two years.

PRESENT TENSE: FORMATION – WEAK VERBS

	Rule	Example
ich	stem + e	parke
du	stem + st	parkst
er, sie, es, man	stem + t	parkt
wir, Sie, sie	stem + en	parken
ihr	stem + t	parkt

EXERCISE

C Insert the correct form of the Present tense.

1 Ich _____ das Schloss mit meiner Kusine. (besuchen)

2 Du _____ die Karten für das Konzert. (bezahlen)

3 Die Dame _____ den Besuchern den Eingang. (zeigen)

4 Wir _____ die Geschichte des Schlosses. (diskutieren)

5 Die Touristen _____ auf die Führung. (warten)

PRESENT TENSE: SPELLING IRREGULARITIES – WEAK/STRONG VERBS

Rule	Example	du	er, sie, es, man
-den, -ten, -tmen, -nen insert e	finden, arbeiten atmen, ordnen	findest, arbeitest, atmest, ordnest	findet, arbeitet, atmet, ordnet
-ßen ,-tzen, -xen, -zen no added s in du form	schließen, putzen, faxen, tanzen	schließt, putzt, faxt, tanzt	schließt, putzt, faxt, tanzt

PRESENT TENSE: -ELN AND -ERN VERBS

	-eln	-ern
ich	klingle	wandere
du	klingelst	wanderst
er, sie, es, man	klingelt	wandert
wir, Sie, sie	klingeln	wandern
ihr	klingelt	wandert

EXERCISE

D Insert the correct form of the Present tense of each verb.

1 Er _____ Mathe schwer. (finden)

2 Frau Braun _____ die Klassenzimmertür sehr laut. (schließen)

3 Paul _____ nicht sehr oft. (antworten)

4 Die Lehrerin _____ an der Tür. (klingeln)

5 Du _____ die Information über den Austausch. (faxen)

PRESENT TENSE: STRONG VERB VOWEL CHANGES

The only changes are to the *du* and *er, sie, es, man* forms. Note that if the stem ends in a sibilant (hissing sound like *sch, ss, tz* or *z*), no *s* is added in the *du* form.

Rule	Examples	du	er, sie, es, man
a > ä	fahren	fährst	fährt
	fallen	fällst	fällt
	fangen	fängst	fängt
	halten	hältst	hält
	laden	lädst	lädt
	lassen	lässt	lässt
	raten	rätst	rät
	schlafen	schläfst	schläft
	wachsen	wächst	wächst
	waschen	wäscht	wäscht
au > äu	laufen	läufst	läuft
e > i	essen	isst	isst
	geben	gibst	gibt
	helfen	hilfst	hilft
	nehmen	nimmst	nimmt
	sprechen	sprichst	spricht
	treten	trittst	tritt
e > ie	befehlen	befiehlst	befiehlt
	empfehlen	empfiehlst	empfiehlt
	lesen	liest	liest
	stehlen	stiehlst	stiehlt
o > ö	stoßen	stößt	stößt

EXERCISE

E Insert the correct form of the Present tense of each verb.

1 Die Assistentin _____ mit den Deutschstunden. (helfen)

2 Er _____ schneller als die anderen Jungs in seiner Klasse. (laufen)

3 Frau Tschärtner _____ Polnisch, Deutsch und Englisch. (sprechen)

4 Wir _____ einen Roman von Christa Wolf. (lesen)

5 Die Geschichtslehrerin _____ den neuen Film über den Holocaust. (empfehlen)

6 Paula _____ ihr Studium sehr ernst. (nehmen)

7 Die Klasse _____ dieses Jahr nach Berlin. (fahren)

8 Mittags _____ ich immer in der Schulkantine. (essen)

9 Die Straßenbahn _____ direkt vor dem Gymnasium. (halten)

10 Meine Freundin _____ mir das Handout. (geben)

PRESENT TENSE MIXED VERBS: ONLY ONE IS IRREGULAR – *WISSEN*

ich	weiß
du	weißt
er, sie, es, man	weiß
wir, Sie, sie	wissen
ihr	wisst

PRESENT TENSE OF *HABEN* AND *SEIN*

	haben	sein
ich	habe	bin
du	hast	bist
er, sie, es, man	hat	ist
wir, Sie, sie	haben	sind
ihr	habt	seid

PRESENT TENSE OF *WERDEN, LASSEN* AND *TUN*

	werden	lassen	tun
ich	werde	lasse	tue
du	wirst	lässt	tust
er, sie, es, man	wird	lässt	tut
wir, Sie, sie	werden	lassen	tun
ihr	werdet	lasst	tut

EXERCISE

F Insert the correct form of the Present tense of each verb.

1 Ich _____ in derselben Partei wie meine Mutter. (sein)

2 Er _____ die Besucher allein. (lassen)

3 Wir _____ schon sehr lange Mitglieder der SPD. (sein)

4 Seine Ideen _____ viel Einfluss auf den Kanzler. (haben)

5 Ich _____, dass sie sich für Politik interessieren. (wissen)

6 Niemand _____ viel von seinen Plänen gehört. (haben)

7 Im Winter _____ es in Berlin kälter als in Bonn. (werden)

8 Er _____ sein Bestes für seine Partei. (tun)

9 Ihr _____ die jüngsten Mitglieder der Partei. (sein)

10 Der Präsident _____, dass es schwer sein wird. (wissen)

PRESENT TENSE: MODAL VERBS

	dürfen	**können**	**mögen**
ich	darf	kann	mag
du	darfst	kannst	magst
er, sie, es, man	darf	kann	mag
wir, Sie, sie	dürfen	können	mögen
ihr	dürft	könnt	mögt

	müssen	**sollen**	**wollen**
ich	muss	soll	will
du	musst	sollst	willst
er, sie, es, man	muss	soll	will
wir, Sie, sie	müssen	sollen	wollen
ihr	müsst	sollt	wollt

EXERCISE

G Insert the correct form of the Present tense of the Modal verbs.

1 Ich _____ viel Obst essen. (müssen)

2 Man _____ hier nicht rauchen. (dürfen)

3 Es _____ schwer sein, fit zu bleiben. (können)

4 Du _____ jeden Morgen joggen. (sollen)

5 Meine Kusine _____ Pommes und Pralinen, aber sie versucht abzunehmen. (mögen)

6 Er _____ jeden Tag zum Sportzentrum gehen. (wollen)

10.4 *Imperative*

Once you have learnt the Present tense, the Imperative is easy. Commands are usually followed by an exclamation mark. In modern German you may find a full stop used instead. The only form where there are any irregularities is the 2nd person familiar singular. Watch out for the strong verbs, which do not add an umlaut in the Imperative.

	Rule	Example	Meaning
2nd person familiar singular	Stem	Sag mir, was du willst.	Tell me what you want.
	Stem + e for verbs with stems ending in -d, -t	Rede nicht so laut! Arbeite schneller!	Don't talk so loudly. Work faster.
	No umlauts added in imperative form of strong verbs	Schlaf gut! Fahr langsamer!	Sleep well. Drive slower.
	Strong verbs where e > i or e > ie do not add e	Gib mir das! Lies das vor!	Give me that. Read that aloud.
1st person plural	Infinitive + *wir*	Sagen wir fünf Uhr.	Let us say five o'clock.
Polite form	Infinitive + *Sie*	Sagen Sie, was Sie denken!	Say what you think.
2nd person familiar plural	Stem + t	Sagt, was ihr wollt.	Say what you want.
	Separable verbs have prefix at end	Steh um 9 auf!	Get up at 9.

EXERCISE

H Give these commands! The infinitive is in brackets.

1 Go left! (gehen)

2 Come in! (hereinkommen)

3 Come back later! (zurückkommen)

4   Go back to the town hall! (zurückgehen)

5   Let's go to town! (gehen)

6   Give me the tickets! (geben – use *du* form)

7   Show me your passport! (zeigen)

8   Get in the bus! (einsteigen)

ONE WORD COMMANDS

There are a number of nouns and other words which you will often hear used as commands. The most common are listed below.

Word	Literal meaning	Meaning of command
Achtung!	Attention.	Watch out!
Bedienung!	Service.	Waiter!
Entschuldigung!	Excuse.	Excuse me.
Feierabend!	End of work.	Knock off work now!
Fräulein!	Miss.	Waitress!
Geradeaus!	Straight on.	Go straight on.
Herein!	Inside.	Come in.
Los!	Away.	Off you go.
Mahlzeit!	Meal.	Enjoy your meal.
Ruhe!	Quiet.	Be quiet.
Schluss!	End.	Stop!
Verzeihung!	Pardon.	Pardon me.
Volltanken!	Fill the tank.	Fill it up.

EXERCISE

1   Which word would be most appropriate?

1   To attract the waiter.

2   To get some peace and quiet.

3   To get petrol.

4   To warn people of danger.

5   To apologize for bumping into somebody.

10.5 *Future tense*

The Future tense is formed with the Present tense of *werden* + Infinitive. The Infinitive goes to the end of the clause. It is not used a lot in German and is reserved for stressing plans for the future. Just as in English, the Present tense is used to describe things people plan to do in the future:

> I'm going to France next summer. *Nächsten Sommer fahre ich nach Frankreich.*

> I will go to France next summer. *Nächsten Sommer werde ich nach Frankreich fahren.*

REMINDER OF THE PRESENT TENSE OF WERDEN

ich	werde
du	wirst
er, sie, es, man	wird
wir, Sie, sie	werden
ihr	werdet

EXERCISE

J Use *werden* to express these plans for the future.

1 I will go to Switzerland.

2 She will buy a ticket.

3 They will go skiing in the Alps.

4 You will see a Swiss play.

5 We will study Switzerland.

10.6 *Uses of* werden

It is important to note the three uses of *werden*:

> *werden* + Adjective = to become sth

> *werden* + Infinitive = Future tense

> *werden* + Past participle = Passive

EXERCISE

K   How is *werden* used here?

1   In den Bergen wird es im Winter sehr kalt.

2   Im Winter werden wir Ski fahren.

3   Letzten Sommer wurde es oft sehr warm.

4   Ich werde im Juli in die Alpen fahren.

5   Im Winter wurde das Dorf abgeschnitten, weil der Schnee so tief war.

6   Unsere Urlaubspläne werden oft schwierig, weil soviele Personen mitfahren.

7   Mein Urlaub wird von einer Reisefirma gebucht.

8   Die Fluglinie wird uns die Tickets schicken.

9   Die Hotels werden zu Weihnachten ausgebucht.

10   Eine Pauschalreise wird billig sein, denke ich.

10.7 *Imperfect tense*

Imperfect tense: use	Example	Meaning
Describe actions which were happening	Es regnete.	It was raining.
Describe things which were done on a regular basis	Donnerstags spielte ich immer Squash.	On Thursdays I always played squash.
Standard past tense of narrative prose	Sie ging hinein.	She went in.
Used for single actions in the past. The general tendency is for Imperfect to be used in writing and Perfect in speech	1400 Menschen protestierten gegen die Extremisten.	1400 people protested against the extremists.
Used with *seit* + Dat. Time phrase for actions which had happened and were still going on	Sie spielte Klavier seit 10 Jahren.	She had been playing the piano for ten years.

NB All verbs, whether weak, strong, mixed, modal or other always have the same form in the 1st Person and 3rd Person Singular.

IMPERFECT TENSE: FORMATION – WEAK VERBS

	Rule	Example
ich	stem + te	parkte
du	stem + test	parktest
er, sie, es, man	stem + te	parkte
wir, Sie, sie	stem + ten	parkten
ihr	stem + tet	parktet

EXERCISE

L   Put the following sentences with Weak verbs into the Imperfect tense.

1   Der Regisseur _____ einen neuen Film. (drehen)

2   Sie _____ viele deutsche Filme. (studieren)

3   Ein Journalist _____ die Filmstars. (fotografieren)

4   Sie _____ den Fassbinder-Film. (kritisieren)

5   Wir _____ vor dem Filmstudio in Babelsberg. (parken)

6   Meine Freundin _____ Klarinette. (spielen)

7   Ihr _____ eine Videokassette. (kaufen)

8   Er _____ als Stuntman. (arbeiten)

IMPERFECT TENSE: FORMATION – STRONG VERBS

	Base form	Example
ich	base form	fiel
du	base form + st	fielst
er, sie, es, man	base form	fiel
wir, Sie, sie	base form + en	fielen
ihr	base form + t	fielt

Since there are a relatively large number of strong verbs it helps to be able to recognize common patterns so you can try to predict the vowel changes for the Imperfect and Past participle. The strong verbs fall into six main groups. The table gives an example of how each verb works. The verbs in brackets (. . .) have the same vowel changes as the others in the group, although the stem vowel of the infinitive is different (e.g. in Group 3, *kommen, kam, gekommen*, cf. *beginnen, begann, begonnen*).

Vowel	Example	Meaning
ei – Stem vowel/Infinitive	leiden	to suffer
i – Stem vowel/Imperfect	er litt	he suffered
i – Stem vowel/Past Participle	er hat gelitten	he has suffered

VERBS MARKED WITH * USUALLY HAVE *SEIN* AS AUXILIARY

Group 1	
ei i i	beißen, greifen, leiden, pfeifen, reißen, reiten*, schneiden, schreiten*
ei ie ie	bleiben*, leihen, schreiben, schreien, schweigen, steigen*, verzeihen
Group 2	
ie o o	biegen*, bieten, fliehen*, fliegen*, fließen*, frieren*, schießen, schließen, verlieren, wiegen
u o o	betrügen, lügen (heben, schwören)
Group 3	
i a u	dringen*, finden, singen, sinken*, springen*, trinken, zwingen
i a o	beginnen, gewinnen, schwimmen* (kommen*)
e a o	befehlen, brechen, empfehlen, helfen, nehmen, sprechen, stehlen, sterben*, treffen, verderben, werfen
Group 4	
e a e	essen, fressen, geben, geschehen*, lesen, messen, sehen, treten*, vergessen
i a e	bitten, sitzen (liegen)
Group 5	
a u a	fahren*, graben, laden, schaffen, schlagen, tragen, wachsen*, waschen
Group 6	
a ie a	fallen*, halten, lassen, raten, schlafen (laufen*)

EXERCISES

M Put each sentence in the Imperfect: Strong verbs Group 1.

1   Er greift sofort zu Aspirin.

2   Er bleibt eine Woche im Bett.

3   Die Mutter schreibt eine Geschichte über ein Krankenhaus.

4   Sie leidet an Asthma.

5   Sie schneidet sich am Arm.

6   Der Arzt steigt in sein Auto ein.

N Put each sentence in the Imperfect: Strong verbs Group 2.

1   Sein Koffer wiegt 20 Kilos.

2   Man schließt die Tür des Flugzeugs.

3   Er fliegt nach München.

4   Die Stewardess bietet ein Getränk und einen Imbiss.

5   Er verliert seine Flugtickets.

6   Die Touristen frieren.

O Put each sentence in the Imperfect: Strong verbs Group 3.

1   Ich finde die Lebkuchen lecker.

2   Er zwingt mich, zum Weihnachtsmarkt zu gehen.

3   Am Marktplatz beginnt die Gruppe, Lieder zu singen.

4   Wir trinken viel Glühwein.

5   Ich gewinne einen Fisch.

6   Der Fisch schwimmt in einem Glas.

7   Sie empfiehlt den Sekt.

8   Ich nehme ein Glas Pfirsichbowle.

9   Wir treffen uns vor der Konzerthalle.

10   Sie sprechen über die wunderbaren Feuerwerke.

P Put each sentence in the Imperfect: Strong verbs Group 4.

1   Was geschieht in der Imbissstube?

2   Ich esse Pizza mit Champignons.

3   Er gibt mir das Rezept.

4   Er vergisst seinen Termin im Wirtshaus.

5   Sie sitzt im Lokal.

Q Put each sentence in the Imperfect: Strong verbs Groups 5 and 6.

1   Die Gewinne wachsen schnell.

2   Der Marketing-Manager fährt nach Frankfurt.

3   Wir halten die Konferenz in dem Messezentrum.

4   Ich lasse meine Dokumente im Büro.

5   Wir raten Ihnen, die Aktien zu verkaufen.

IMPERFECT TENSE: FORMATION – MIXED VERBS

	Base form	Example
ich	base form	brachte
du	base form + st	brachtest
er, sie, es, man	base form	brachte
wir, Sie, sie	base form + n	brachten
ihr	base form + t	brachtet

IMPERFECT TENSE AND PAST PARTICIPLE: MIXED VERBS

Mixed verbs add elements to the stem but also have vowel and/or consonant changes to the stem when forming the Imperfect and Past participle. These verbs have *-te* at the end of the Imperfect and *-t* at the end of the past participle.

Infinitive	Imperfect	Past Participle
brennen	brannte	gebrannt
bringen	brachte	gebracht
denken	dachte	gedacht
kennen	kannte	gekannt
nennen	nannte	genannt
rennen	rannte	gerannt (takes *sein* as auxiliary)
senden	sandte	gesandt
wenden	wandte	gewandt
wissen	wusste	gewusst

EXERCISE

R Insert the correct form of the Imperfect tense.

1 Die Museumsdirektorin _____ mir ein paar Prospekte. (senden)

2 Das war schön, weil ich die Stadt gar nicht _____. (kennen)

3 Mein Freund _____ ein paar Sehenswürdigkeiten, die ich besuchen könnte. (nennen)

4 Ich _____, dass das neue Museum vielleicht von Interesse ist. (denken)

5 Ich _____ nicht, wie viel der Eintritt kostet. (wissen)

IMPERFECT TENSE: IRREGULAR FORMS

The Imperfect tense of *haben* and *sein* are used to form the Pluperfect tense. (See 10.10.)

	haben	sein
ich	hatte	war
du	hattest	warst
er, sie, es, man	hatte	war
wir, Sie, sie	hatten	waren
ihr	hattet	wart

IMPERFECT TENSE: MODAL VERBS

Note that none of the Modal verbs have an umlaut in the Imperfect tense.

	dürfen	können	mögen
ich	durfte	konnte	mochte
du	durftest	konntest	mochtest
er, sie, es, man	durfte	konnte	mochte
wir, Sie, sie	durften	konnten	mochten
ihr	durftet	konntet	mochtet

	müssen	sollen	wollen
ich	musste	sollte	wollte
du	musstest	solltest	wolltest
er, sie, es, man	musste	sollte	wollte
wir, Sie, sie	mussten	sollten	wollten
ihr	musstet	solltet	wolltet

EXERCISE

S Insert the correct form of the Imperfect tense of each modal verb.

1 Er _____ hier parken. (dürfen)

2 Wir _____ uns verkleiden. (müssen)

3 Du _____ ihn kontaktieren. (können)

4 Meine Geschwister _____ uns zu Ostern besuchen. (wollen)

5 Meine Großmutter _____ zur Hochzeit kommen. (sollen)

10.8 *Perfect tense*

Use of Perfect tense	Example	Meaning
Corresponds to English 'have done sth'	Sie haben eine Marktnische gefunden.	They have found a corner in the market.
Used for single actions in the past in spoken German (particularly in S. Germany and Austria).	Wir haben unsere Freunde besucht.	We visited our friends.

Verbs form the Perfect tense either with the auxiliary *haben* or *sein*. (See 10.9.) The past participle goes to the end of the clause.

PERFECT TENSE: FORMATION – WEAK VERBS

To form the past participle of Weak verbs take the stem and add the prefix *ge-* and suffix *-t*. The exceptions listed below do *not* add the prefix *ge-*.

Rule	Example	Meaning
Verbs with inseparable prefix *be-, er-, miss-, ver-, zer-*	Er hat es verkauft.	He sold it.
Verbs with separable prefix *vor-*	Sie hat es vorbereitet.	She prepared it.
-ieren verbs (apart from *frieren* and *verlieren* which are strong verbs)	Sie haben es analysiert.	They analysed it.
-eien verbs	Er hat es prophezeit.	He prophesied it.

EXERCISE

T　Insert the correct form of the Perfect tense of each weak verb. All use *haben* as Auxiliary.

1　Der Koch _____ die Forelle _____. (vorbereiten)

2　Er _____ meine Kochkenntnisse _____. (diskutieren)

3　Die Verkäuferin _____ verschiedene Brotsorten _____. (verkaufen)

4　Du _____ zu viel Obst _____. (kaufen)

5　Ihr _____ die Kalorien _____ (zählen)

10.9 haben *or* sein *as auxiliary?*

See tables of Strong and Mixed verbs above for the Past Participles. There are a number of useful rules which help you remember whether to use *haben* or *sein* as Auxiliary.

Verbs with sein	Verbs	Example
Intransitive verbs of motion	*fallen, gehen, kommen, laufen, springen* and lots more	Sie ist ins Wasser gefallen. Er ist in die Stadt gegangen.
Intransitive verbs indicating a change of state	*einschlafen* *explodieren* *frieren* *schmelzen* *sterben*	Helga ist eingeschlafen. Das Auto ist explodiert. Das Wasser ist gefroren. Das Eis ist geschmolzen. Die Tänzerin ist gestorben.
Certain commonly used verbs take *sein*	*bleiben* *sein* *werden*	Sie sind lange da geblieben. Hier ist es schön gewesen. Dort ist es kälter geworden.
Verbs meaning to happen/occur	*geschehen* *passieren* *vorkommen*	Was ist hier geschehen? Nichts ist passiert. Was ist hier vorgekommen?
Verbs meaning to succeed or fail	*gelingen* *misslingen*	Es ist mir gelungen. Es ist ihm misslungen.

NB Remember that if used transitively, verbs of motion such as *fahren* or *fliegen* form compound tenses with *haben*.

Use	Verbs of motion	Example	Meaning
Intransitive	Use *sein* for compound tenses	Sie *ist* nach Berlin geflogen.	She flew to Berlin.
Transitive	Use *haben* for compound tenses	Sie *hat* Peter nach Hause gefahren.	She drove Peter home.

REMINDER OF THE PRESENT TENSE OF THE AUXILIARY VERBS *HABEN* AND *SEIN*

	haben	sein
ich	habe	bin
du	hast	bist
er, sie, es, man	hat	ist
wir, Sie, sie	haben	sind
ihr	habt	seid

EXERCISES

U Insert the correct form of *haben* or *sein* in each sentence.

1 Die Situation _____ kompliziert geworden.

2 Ein Auto _____ explodiert.

3 Ich _____ in die Tschechische Republik gefahren.

4 Nicht viel _____ in den Ferien passiert.

5 Sie _____ die Touristen nach Belgien geflogen.

6 Wann _____ sie aufgestanden?

7 Wann _____ Sie in die Stadt gefahren?

8 Was _____ Sie heute gemacht?

9 Was _____ du zum Frühstück gegessen?

10 Wie _____ du hierhergekommen?

V Strong verbs. Put each of the sentences in the exercises M–Q on pp. 111–112 into the Perfect tense.

W Mixed verbs. (Revise p. 113) Put each sentence in the Perfect tense. All take *haben*.

1 Wir denken an die neue Generation.

2 Ich sende die Informationen.

3 Er wendet sich an den Bürgermeister.

4 Er bringt sie nach Hause.

5 Ich kenne die Altstadt sehr gut.

6 Er weiß alles über die Geschichte der Stadt.

7 Sie nennen einige interessante Aspekte der Geschichte.

8 Ich denke an die guten alten Zeiten.

PERFECT TENSE: MODAL VERBS

Normally Modal verbs have the infinitive as Past participle. For three Modal verbs there are two forms of Past participle. The choice is simple.

Rule	Example	Meaning
Modal verbs *können, mögen* and *wollen* used on their own have a Participle ending in *-t*.	Ich habe es *gekonnt*. Sie hat es *gemocht*. Er hat es *gewollt*.	I was able to do it. She liked it. He wanted it.
All modal verbs used with an infinitive have their own infinitive as participle.	Wir haben es machen *wollen*. Sie haben es trinken *dürfen*.	We wanted to do it. They have been allowed to drink it.

EXERCISE

X   Put each sentence into German, using the Perfect tense of a Modal verb.

1   They wanted to see it.

2   I wanted it.

3   He has been able to visit the park.

4   She has been supposed to write a diary.

5   Did you like the package holiday?

10.10 *Pluperfect, Future Perfect and Conditional Perfect*

Since all these tenses use the Auxiliary and Past participle they give you further practice in the use of *haben* or *sein* as Auxiliary. There are no exceptions to the rules at all.

PLUPERFECT

The Pluperfect corresponds to *had* + Past participle in English. (See also Imperfect + *seit* – 10.7.) It is used to describe actions which came before other actions in the past. It is formed with the Imperfect of *haben* or *sein* + Past participle. The Past participle goes to the end of the clause. There are no exceptions.

	Imperfect of *haben*	Imperfect of *sein*	+ Past participle
ich	hatte	war	
du	hattest	warst	
er, sie, es, man	hatte	war	
wir, Sie, sie	hatten	waren	
ihr	hattet	wart	

EXERCISE

Y   Revise rules on Past participles and Auxiliaries and insert the correct forms of the
Pluperfect tense.

1   Der Urlaub _____ im Dezember _____. (beginnen)

2   Herr Boos _____ nach New York _____. (fliegen)

3   Seine Frau _____ einen Billigflug _____. (reservieren)

4   Er _____ seinen Stadtplan _____. (verlieren)

5   Beide _____ das Hotel ganz leicht _____. (finden)

6   Zuerst _____ sie nicht gut _____. (schlafen)

7   Am folgenden Morgen _____ sie in einen Bus _____. (einsteigen)

8   Sie _____ die Hauptsehenswürdigkeiten _____. (sehen)

9   Jemand _____ von einem Hochhaus _____. (fallen)

10   Die Polizei _____ schnell _____. (ankommen)

FUTURE PERFECT

This corresponds to 'will have' + Past participle. Use the Present tense of *werden* and
the Perfect Infinitive. This tense is not used much in English or German, but it is
useful to be able to recognize it.

Present tense of *werden*	+ Perfect infinitive
ich werde	gespielt haben/gegangen sein
du wirst	
er, sie, es, man wird	
wir, Sie, sie werden	
ihr werdet	

Example	Meaning
Bis zum Ende der Woche werden sie sechs Burgen besucht haben.	They will have visited six castles by the end of the week.
Ich werde nach Magdeburg gefahren sein, bevor sie abfahren.	I will have gone to Magdeburg before you leave.

The Present tense is often used in German to indicate that events will have been
completed by a specific time, e.g. I will have finished it by Friday. *Bis Freitag bin ich
fertig.*

EXERCISE

Z   Translate the following sentences into German.

1   They will have invested DM2000.

2   He will have visited the firm in Germany.

3   They will have found a new marketing manager.

4   She will have developed a new product.

5   I will have finished the project by September.

CONDITIONAL PERFECT: 'WOULD HAVE . . .'

Conditional tense of *werden*	+ Perfect infinitive
ich würde	gespielt haben/gegangen sein
du würdest	
er, sie, es, man würde	
wir, Sie, sie würden	
ihr würdet	

NB this is rarely used. People tend to use the Pluperfect Subjunctive (Konjunktiv II *Ich hätte gespielt/ich wäre gegangen.* See 10.11 and 10.20.)

10.11 *Conditional sentences*

There are three types of conditional sentences. They normally involve *wenn* (if) with the main verb at the end of the end of the clause. (See Chapter 3 on omission of *wenn*.)

Rule	Example	Meaning
1. Open conditions involve *wenn* + Present tense, and Present tense in the other half of the sentence.	Wenn es *regnet, bleibe* ich zu Hause.	If it rains I will stay at home.
2. Unreal conditions involve *wenn* + Imperfect Subjunctive, and Conditional tense or Imperfect Subjunctive (if less clumsy) in other half of the sentence.	Wenn es kalt *wäre, würde* ich nicht *ausgehen.* Wenn ich Zeit *hätte, wäre* es schön, Sie zu sehen.	If it was/were cold I would not go out. If I had time it would be nice to see you.
3. Lost chances involve *wenn* + Pluperfect Subjunctive in both clauses.	Wenn ich das Geld *gehabt hätte, wäre* ich in die Stadt *gefahren.*	If I had had the money I would have gone to town.

Conditional tense – use the Imperfect Subjunctive of *werden* + infinitive. There are no exceptions.

IMPERFECT SUBJUNCTIVE OF *WERDEN*

ich	würde
du	würdest
er, sie, es, man	würde
wir, Sie, sie	würden
ihr	würdet

Pluperfect Subjunctive – formed with the Imperfect Subjunctive of either *haben* or *sein* + Past participle. There are no exceptions. These forms are very common.

	Imperfect Subjunctive of *haben*	Imperfect Subjunctive of *sein*
ich	hätte	wäre
du	hättest	wärst
er, sie, es, man	hätte	wäre
wir, Sie, sie	hätten	wären
ihr	hättet	wäret

IMPERFECT SUBJUNCTIVE

In the case of Weak verbs there is no difference between the Indicative and the Subjunctive of the imperfect. The Strong verbs are more noticeably different.

	Weak verbs	Strong verbs	Strong verbs + umlaut if possible
ich	kaufte	ginge	käme
du	kauftest	gingest	kämest
er, sie, es, man	kaufte	ginge	käme
wir, Sie, sie	kauften	gingen	kämen
ihr	kauftet	ginget	kämet

IMPERFECT SUBJUNCTIVE: MODAL VERBS ADDING UMLAUT

Sollen and *wollen* do not add umlauts.

	dürfen	können	mögen	müssen
ich	dürfte	könnte	möchte	müsste
du	dürftest	könntest	möchtest	müsstest
er, sie, es, man	dürfte	könnte	möchte	müsste
wir, Sie, sie	dürften	könnten	möchten	müssten
ihr	dürftet	könntet	möchtet	müsstet

IMPERFECT SUBJUNCTIVE: MIXED VERBS ADDING UMLAUT

Only *bringen* and *wissen* add umlauts. The other mixed verbs do not add umlauts.

	bringen	wissen
ich	brächte	wüsste
du	brächtest	wüsstest
er, sie, es, man	brächte	wüsste
wir, Sie, sie	brächten	wüssten
ihr	brächtet	wüsstet

EXERCISES

A Are the following open conditions, unreal conditions or lost chances?

1 I would go to town if I had time.

2 If it is snowy I will not go shopping.

3 I would have visited my aunt if I had known her address.

4 They will use the car more when they are older.

5 We would go swimming more if the pool was nearer.

B Translate the following conditional sentences into German.

1 I would go to the baker's if they sold fresh rolls.

2 She will buy the coat if it is cheap.

3 She would have bought a film if the shop had been open.

4 The vases would have been cheaper if you had bought them in Poland.

5   They will go to the department store if they have time.

6   They would buy an umbrella if it was raining.

7   They would have given us tickets if they had known.

8   We would go to the concert if it were possible.

10.12 *Participles, present and past and their use*

The Present participle is formed by adding -*d* to the infinitive. The formation of the Past participle has already been outlined in 10.8.

Rule	Example	Meaning
Present participles are often used as adjectives	Das ist *überraschend*.	That is surprising.
Many Past participles are used as adjectives.	Er war *verletzt*.	He was injured.
Present and Past participles may form part of adjectival phrases. These are usually translated into English as relative clauses.	Kirsten ist die am Fenster *sitzende* Frau.	Kirsten is the woman sitting at the window. (Lit. Kirsten is the at the window sitting woman.)
	Das ist mein im Sommer *gekauftes* Auto.	That is my car which I bought in the summer.

EXERCISE

C   Translate the following sentences into English.

1   Wir haben die im Wasser schwimmenden Enten gesehen.

2   Die Eier suchenden Kinder sind sehr glücklich.

3   Die letzte Woche gebackenen Kekse schmecken super.

4   Die schön verpackten Geschenke sind von meiner Mutter.

5   Haben Sie das zerbrochene Fenster gesehen?

TRANSLATING THE ENGLISH –*ING*

Rule	Example	Meaning
Use *während* + verb for an action while another is happening.	Während ich in die Stadt ging, sah ich einen Unfall.	Going into town I saw an accident.
Use Infinitive after verbs of seeing and hearing.	Ich sah/hörte den Bus kommen.	I saw/heard the bus coming.

Rule	Example	Meaning
Use Past participle after *kommen*.	Sie kam hierhergelaufen.	She came running here.
Use verb + *weiter* for actions which continue.	Sie spielten weiter.	They kept on playing.
Use *ohne* + *zu* + Infinitive for 'without' + ing.	Ohne lange zu warten, ging sie in die Bibliothek.	She went into the library without waiting for long.
Use *bevor/nachdem* + verb for before/after + ing.	Bevor/Nachdem wir die Karten gekauft hatten, gingen wir Eis essen.	Before/After buying the tickets we went for an ice-cream.

TRANSLATING *BEFORE* AND *AFTER*

Rule	Example	Meaning
Conjunction – bevor/ nachdem	Bevor/Nachdem sie es gesehen hatten, wollten sie es haben.	Before/After seeing it they wanted to have it.
Preposition – vor/nach	Before/After breakfast they went for a walk.	Vor/Nach dem Frühstück gingen sie spazieren.
Adverb – vorher/nachher.	Vorher/Nachher spielten wir viel besser.	Before that/Afterwards we played much better.

EXERCISES

D   Put each sentence into German.

1   While visiting Goslar I saw a friend.

2   We saw a tram coming.

3   It kept on raining.

4   Without thinking much we went into an expensive restaurant.

5   After buying the guide-book we walked round the castle.

E   Insert the correct word for 'before' or 'after' in each sentence.

1   Sie sahen meinen Chef, _____ er nach Amerika ging. (before)

2   Wir sprachen _____ über die Marketing-Probleme. (before)

3   Ich arbeitete _____ der Wende in Weimar. (after)

4   Sie investierte viel Geld, _____ sie die Firma recherchiert hatte. (after)

5   Er versprach es, _____ er viel über die Produkte wusste. (before)

10.13 Passive

The Active voice tells us clearly who is doing the actions, e.g. *Die Frau reserviert die Karten*. The Passive voice tells us what is going on, but does not necessarily say who is doing it. *Die Karten werden (von der Frau) reserviert.*

There are two Passives in German. The Passive with *werden* describes a process. The Passive with *sein* expresses a fixed state.

The Passive is used to describe a process which is happening or happened. Use the appropriate tense of *werden* and the Past participle.

Tense	Form of *werden*	Example	Meaning
Present	Present tense	es wird gesagt	it is said
Future	Present tense	es wird gesagt	it will be said
Imperfect	Imperfect tense	es wurde gesagt	it was said
Perfect	Perfect tense	es ist gesagt worden	it has been said
Pluperfect tense	Pluperfect tense	es war gesagt worden	it had been said

Rule	Example	Meaning
Passive describes a process. Use *von* for the person/agent who/which did the action.	Das Fenster wurde gestern von den Kindern gebrochen.	The window was broken yesterday by the children.
Verbs taking the Dative can't be used in the Passive. Use *man* and Active mood.	Man half ihm, es zu machen.	He was helped to do it.
Use Passive with *sein* to describe a fixed state. Past participles are used like adjectives.	Das Fenster war gebrochen.	The window was broken. (This describes a state of events.)
Use the Reflexive Pronoun with *lassen* + Infinitive to express the Passive.	Das lässt sich leicht erklären.	That is easily explained.
Use *zu* + Infinitive after *es gibt* to express the Passive Infinitive.	Es gibt viel zu besprechen.	There is a lot to be discussed

EXERCISES

F   Translate the following sentences into English.

   1   Der Geburtstagskuchen wurde am Montag gebacken.

   2   Die Karten für das Rock-Konzert wurden gestern abgeschickt.

    3   Die Geschenke sind vorgestern abgeholt worden.

    4   Die Ostereier wurden von den Kindern gemalt.

    5   Viele Eier wurden gefunden.

    6   Das Faschingsgeschäft war am Sonntag geschlossen.

    7   Das lässt sich schnell machen.

    8   Es gibt viele Kostüme zu sehen.

    9   Viele Menschen wurden kritisiert.

  10   Das lässt sich schwer erklären.

G   Translate the following sentences into German.

    1   The tickets for the concert were booked by my father.

    2   The boutique was closed.

    3   She was helped by the salesgirl.

    4   There is a lot to be seen.

    5   Many people were injured in the new shopping centre.

10.14 *Use of infinitives*

Rule	Example	Meaning
Don't use *zu* with Infinitives after Modal verbs.	Wir können Ihre Probleme verstehen.	We can understand your problems.
Don't use *zu* with Infinitives after verbs of perception and *lassen*	Ich sehe sie kommen. Wir lassen sie da stehen.	I see them coming. We leave them standing there.
zu + Infinitive is the norm	Er versucht, es zu bestellen. Wir hoffen, es zu machen.	He tries to order it. We hope to do it.
Use *um* + *zu* + Infinitive for 'in order to . . .'	Sie fuhren nach Essen, um die Firma zu besuchen.	They went to Essen to visit the firm.
Use *zu* + Infinitive after adjectives	Das ist schwer zu erklären.	That is hard to explain.
Use *zu* + Infinitive after *ohne/statt* + English '-ing'	Sie entwickelten es, ohne viel Geld auszugeben. Sie kauften es, statt es zu mieten.	They developed it without spending much money. They bought it instead of hiring it.

EXERCISE

H   Translate the following sentences into German.

1   They want to swim.

2   I hope to play tennis.

3   They saw him playing hockey.

4   They went to Wolfsburg to visit the firm.

5   She did it without going to the sports centre.

10.15 *Use of Modal verbs and* lassen *with infinitives*

The Modal verbs and *lassen* (to have something done) are used with infinitives without *zu*. There are a number of occasions when the meaning does not correspond exactly to the 'usual' definition.

Verb – usual meaning	Other usage	Meaning
dürfen – to be allowed to	Man darf hier nicht rauchen.	You cannot/must not/are not allowed to smoke here.
können – to be able to	Das kann möglich sein. Er kann jeden Moment ankommen.	That may be possible. He may arrive at any moment.
mögen – to like to	Das mag unangenehm sein, aber es ist nötig.	That may be unpleasant, but it is necessary.
müssen – to have to	Muss das sein? Sie muss bald hier sein. Das Parkhaus muss in der Nähe sein.	Is that really necessary? She's bound to be here soon. The multi-storey car park ought to be near here.
sollen – to be supposed to	Sie sollen das Fenster schließen.	I want you to shut the window.
wollen – to want to	Wir wollen in die USA fahren. Wollen Sie das bitte lauter sagen? Er will Sie gesehen haben.	We're going to go to the USA. Would you say it louder please? He claims to have seen you.
lassen – to let, allow	Sie liessen es renovieren. Das lässt sich leicht reparieren.	They had it renovated. That can easily be repaired.

NB Note the difference in meaning between *sie darf nicht spielen*, she must not play, and *sie muss nicht spielen*, she doesn't have to play/she needn't play.

EXERCISE

1   Translate the following sentences into German.

    1   May I park here?

    2   We can take a taxi.

    3   She may visit the firm at any time.

    4   They want to go to the theatre.

    5   They would like to do a city tour.

    6   They have to reserve tickets.

    7   The cathedral ought to be near here.

    8   We are going to visit the zoo.

    9   They are supposed to go to the tourist information office.

  10   Can you tell me where it is?

10.16 *Impersonal verbs*

These verbs cannot have a personal subject. Most are to do with weather (first in the list), happening, succeeding and failing. Some verbs have a separate meaning when used impersonally (with *es* as subject).

Verb used Impersonally	Meaning	Example	Meaning
blitzen	to lighten	Es blitzt.	There is lightning.
donnern	to thunder	Es donnert.	There is thunder.
hageln	to hail	Es hagelte.	It was hailing.
regnen	to rain	Es regnet.	It is raining.
schneien	to snow	Es schneit.	It is snowing.
auffallen + Dat.	to strike sb	Es fällt mir auf, dass es teuer ist.	It strikes me that it is dear.
einfallen + Dat.	to occur to sb	Es fällt mir ein, dass es spät ist.	It occurs to me that it is late.
geben + Acc.	to be	Es gibt 4 Kinos.	There are four cinemas.
gehen	to be (fine, bad, etc.)	Es geht mir gut/ schlecht.	I am fine/feeling bad.
gehen + um + Acc.	to be about	Es geht um den Kanzler.	It is about the Chancellor.

Verb used Impersonally	Meaning	Example	Meaning
gelingen	to succeed	Es gelingt mir.	I succeed.
handeln + von + Dat.	to be about	Es handelt von einem Filmstar.	It's about a film star.
leid tun + Dat.	to regret, be sorry	Es tut mir leid.	I am sorry, I regret.
passen	to suit	Es passt mir.	It suits me.
schmecken	to taste	Es schmeckt mir gut.	It tastes good to me.
sein	to be/feel	Es ist mir warm.	I am/feel warm.
stehen	to suit	Der Hut steht mir gut.	The hat suits me.

EXERCISE

J Translate the following sentences into German.

1 She is cold.

2 The raincoat suits her.

3 It was snowing yesterday.

4 They succeeded.

5 We are fine.

10.17 *Reflexive verbs*

There are ten commonly used 'true' reflexive verbs in German which are **only** used with a reflexive pronoun. (See Chapter 7 for more on Reflexive Pronouns.)

Reflexive Verb	Meaning
sich bedanken bei + Dat.	to say thank you to sb
sich beeilen	to hurry
sich befinden	to be situated, find oneself
sich benehmen	to behave
sich entschließen	to decide
sich erholen	to recover (from illness, etc.)
sich erkälten	to catch cold
sich irren	to be mistaken
sich verabschieden	to take one's leave
sich weigern	to refuse (to do sth)

Reflexive verbs have reflexive pronouns. Most use the Accusative, but occasionally the Dative of the reflexive is used if there are two objects, one direct and one indirect. All these verbs form compound tenses with *haben*.

EXERCISE

K   Complete each sentence with the correct Reflexive verb and Pronoun.

1   Sie _____ _____, den Bundestag zu besuchen. (decided)

2   Wir _____ _____ beim Abgeordneten. (thanked)

3   Die Mitglieder der Protestgruppe _____ _____, weil das Wetter so schlecht war. (caught cold)

4   Die norwegische Botschaft _____ _____ in Berlin. (is located)

5   Der Minister _____ _____, mehr zum Thema zu sagen. (refused)

10.18 *Verbs with cases*

The verbs *sein*, *bleiben* and *werden* are followed by the Nominative case. Almost all other verbs are followed by the Accusative case. There are quite a number of verbs followed by the Dative case. The following are the most common. Note that some Impersonal verbs are followed by Dative. (See 10.16.)

Verb + Dative	Meaning	Example	Meaning
ähneln	to resemble	Er ähnelt seinem Bruder.	He resembles his brother.
sich anpassen	to adapt to	Er passt sich den anderen an.	He adapts to the others.
ausweichen	to avoid	Sie weicht ihm aus.	She avoids him.
befehlen	to order	Ich befehle ihm, es zu machen.	I order him to do it.
begegnen	to meet	Wir begegnen den Gästen.	We meet the guests.
danken	to thank	Ich danke Ihnen im Namen der Gruppe.	I thank you in the name of the group.
drohen	to threaten	Sie droht ihm mit Entlassung.	She threatens him with dismissal.
entkommen	to escape from sb	Sie ist der Gefahr entkommen.	She escaped the danger.
erlauben	to allow	Ich erlaube Ihnen, mit dem Computer zu arbeiten.	I allow you to work with the computer.

Verb + Dative	Meaning	Example	Meaning
folgen	to follow	Sie folgt ihnen.	She follows them.
gefallen	to please	Es gefällt ihr.	She likes it. (lit. it pleases her)
gehorchen	to obey	Ich gehorche ihnen.	I obey them.
gehören	to belong to	Das gehört ihr.	That belongs to her.
gratulieren	to congratulate	Ich gratuliere dir.	I congratulate you.
helfen	to help	Sie helfen uns.	They help us.
imponieren	to impress	Er imponierte mir.	He impressed me.
schaden	to damage	Das schadet der Umwelt.	That is damaging the environment.
schmeicheln	to flatter	Sie schmeicheln ihm.	They flatter him.
trauen	to trust	Ich traue ihm.	I trust him.
verzeihen	to forgive	Wir verzeihen ihnen.	We forgive them.
weh tun	to hurt	Es tut mir weh.	It hurts me.
widersprechen	to contradict	Sie widersprach ihm.	She contradicted him.
zustimmen	to agree	Sie stimmen ihm zu.	They agree with him.

EXERCISE

L   Translate the following sentences into German.

1   They helped their colleagues.

2   He followed the boss.

3   She liked the product.

4   The computer belonged to me.

5   They succeeded in exporting to Poland.

6   He contradicted his lawyer. (der Anwalt = lawyer)

7   The new building impressed the secretary.

8   They met their new colleagues.

9   She flattered the workers.

10   We trusted the manager.

10.19 *Verbs followed by prepositions*

There are large numbers of verbs which are followed by certain prepositions. It may help to learn them in groups. The more you use them, the more familiar they become. They are listed in alphabetical order of the prepositions which follow them.

VERBS FOLLOWED BY *AN* OR *AUF*

Infinitive	Preposition + Case	Meaning
denken	an + Acc.	to think about
erinnern	an + Acc.	to remind of
sich erinnern	an + Acc.	to remember (about)
sich gewöhnen	an + Acc.	to get used to
glauben	an + Acc.	to believe in
erkennen	an + Dat.	to recognize by
fehlen (Impersonal)	an + Dat.	to be lacking in
leiden	an + Dat.	to suffer from
sterben	an + Dat.	to die of
teilnehmen	an + Dat.	to take part in
vorbeigehen	an + Dat.	to go past
achten	auf + Acc.	to pay attention to
anspielen	auf + Acc.	to allude to
antworten	auf + Acc.	to reply to
aufpassen	auf + Acc.	to pay attention to
sich beschränken	auf + Acc.	to restrict oneself to
bestehen	auf + Acc.	to insist on
sich beziehen	auf + Acc.	to refer to
sich freuen	auf + Acc.	to look forward to
hoffen	auf + Acc.	to hope for
sich konzentrieren	auf + Acc.	to concentrate on
reagieren	auf + Acc.	to react to
trinken	auf + Acc.	to drink to
sich verlassen	auf + Acc.	to rely on
verzichten	auf + Acc.	to do without
sich vorbereiten	auf + Acc.	to prepare for
warten	auf + Acc.	to wait for
zählen	auf + Acc.	to count on
basieren	auf + Dat.	to be based on

EXERCISE

M *an* or *auf*? Insert the correct preposition in each sentence.

1 Es erinnert mich _____ meine Kindheit.

2 Wir achten _____ die Zeit.

3 Ich gewöhne mich _____ die Methoden.

4 Er antwortet _____ die Frage.

5 Es fehlt _____ Musik.

6 Es basiert _____ Informationen aus dem Internet.

7 Sie ist _____ Lungenkrebs gestorben.

8 Wir warten _____ die neuen CDs.

9 Sie ging _____ der Kirche vorbei.

10 Ich muss mich _____ die Hauptprobleme konzentrieren.

VERBS FOLLOWED BY *AUS, BEI, FÜR, IN OR MIT*

Infinitive	Preposition + case	Meaning
bestehen	aus + Dat.	to consist of
sich beklagen	bei + Dat.	to complain to
sich beschweren	bei + Dat.	to complain to sb
sich entschuldigen	bei + Dat.	to apologize to sb
sich entscheiden für	für + Acc.	to decide in favour of
halten	für + Acc.	to consider (sth to be sth)
sich interessieren	für + Acc.	to be interested in
schwärmen	für + Acc.	to rave about
sorgen	für + Acc.	to care for
investieren	in + Acc.	to invest in
sich beschäftigen	mit + Dat.	to occupy oneself with sth
rechnen	mit + Dat.	to reckon with
telefonieren	mit + Dat.	to telephone sb

EXERCISE

N   *Aus/bei/für/in/mit?* Insert the correct preposition in each sentence.

1   Es besteht _____ vielen Teilen.

2   Er bedankt sich _____ die Hilfe.

3   Sie müssen _____ die neue Technologie investieren.

4   Sie interessieren sich _____ Computer.

5   Sie haben _____ Frau Bauer telefoniert.

6 Ich halte das _____ eine gute Idee.

7 Er entschuldigte sich _____ mir.

8 Sie sorgen _____ die technischen Details.

9 Er hat sich _____ den neuen Produkten beschäftigt.

10 Sie sorgt _____ die Qualität der Produkte.

VERBS FOLLOWED BY NACH, ÜBER, UM, UNTER, VON, VOR OR ZU

Infinitive	Preposition + Case	Meaning
sich erkundigen	nach + Dat.	to enquire about
fragen	nach + Dat.	to ask about
greifen	nach + Dat.	to reach for
riechen	nach + Dat.	to smell of
schmecken	nach + Dat.	to taste of
sehnen	nach + Dat.	to long for
suchen	nach + Dat.	to look for
verlangen	nach + Dat.	to demand
sich amüsieren	über + Acc.	to be amused about
sich ärgern	über + Acc.	to get annoyed with
sich beklagen	über + Acc.	to complain about
sich beschweren	über + Acc.	to complain about
lachen	über + Acc.	to laugh about
nachdenken	über + Acc.	to ponder on
sich streiten	über + Acc.	to quarrel about
sich unterhalten	über + Acc.	to chat about
sich wundern	über + Acc.	to be surprised at
sich bewerben	um + Acc.	to apply for
bitten	um + Acc.	to ask for
gehen (Impersonal)	um + Acc.	to concern
kämpfen	um + Acc.	to fight for
sich kümmern	um + Acc.	to worry about
sich sorgen	um + Acc.	to worry about
trauern	um + Acc.	to mourn for
leiden	unter + Dat.	to suffer from

Infinitive	Preposition + Case	Meaning
verstehen	unter + Dat	to understand by sth
abhängen	von + Dat.	to depend on
sich erholen	von + Dat.	to recover from
erzählen	von + Dat.	to talk about
halten	von + Dat.	to think of (to rate sth)
handeln (Impersonal)	von + Dat.	to deal with
reden	von + Dat.	to talk about
sich verabschieden	von + Dat.	to take one's leave of
fliehen	vor + Dat.	to flee from
retten	vor + Dat.	to rescue from
schützen	vor + Dat.	to protect from
sich verstecken	vor + Dat.	to hide from
warnen	vor + Dat.	to warn of
beitragen	zu + Dat.	to contribute to
neigen	zu + Dat.	to be prone to
überreden	zu + Dat.	to persuade to

EXERCISE

Nach/über/um/unter/von/vor or zu? Insert the correct preposition in each sentence.

1 Viele Teenager halten nicht viel _____ Drogenberatungsstellen.

2 Andere wundern sich _____ die vielen Leute, die Tabletten schlucken.

3 Wenn Leute _____ Drogen abhängen, ist es sehr schwer, weil sie immer Geld brauchen.

4 Einige leiden _____ Essstörungen und werden sehr krank.

5 Lehrer warnen _____ den Gefahren.

6 Man versucht, Süchtige _____ einem Rehabilitationsprogramm zu überreden.

7 Viele Jugendliche greifen zu schnell _____ Drogen.

8 Oft beschweren sie sich _____ den Mangel an Freizeitaktivitäten.

9 Sie sehnen _____ einem interessanteren Leben.

10 Was verstehen wir _____ interessant? Schwer zu sagen.

10.20 *Subjunctive mood and indirect speech*

The most commonly used forms are the Present, Imperfect, Perfect and Pluperfect tense. There are no vowel changes in the Present tense. There are no irregular forms in the Mixed verbs or Modal verbs.

The hardest form is perhaps the Imperfect Subjunctive, because some Strong and Mixed verbs add an umlaut, but even this is not too difficult! Many forms of the Subjunctive are identical to the Indicative forms. For Indirect speech, the aim is to use a form which is clearly different from the Indicative, if at all possible.

The Subjunctive mood is used for conditional sentences (see 10.10 and 10.11) and for indirect speech, but is becoming less common in spoken language.

	Present Subjunctive Weak verb	**Present Subjunctive Strong Verb**
ich + stem + e	parke	gebe
du + stem + est	parkest	gebest
er, sie, es, man + stem + e	parke	gebe
wir, Sie, sie + stem + en	parken	geben
ihr + stem + et	parket	gebet

	Present Subjunctive *haben*	**Present Subjunctive *sein***
ich + stem + e	habe	sei
du + stem + est	habest	seiest
er, sie, es, man + stem + e	habe	sei
wir, Sie, sie + stem + en	haben	seien
ihr + stem + et	habet	seiet

The Imperfect Subjunctive is identical to the Imperfect Indicative, so is usually avoided.

	Imperfect Subjunctive Weak verbs = same as Indicative	**Imperfect Subjunctive Strong Verbs – take Imperfect Indicative and add endings**
ich	kaufte	ginge
du	kauftest	gingest
er, sie, es, man	kaufte	ginge
wir, Sie, sie	kauften	gingen
ihr	kauftet	ginget

The only common verbs which have an umlaut in the Imperfect Subjunctive are:

Infinitive	Imperfect Subjunctive
finden	fände
geben	gäbe
haben	hätte
kommen	käme
sein	wäre
tun	täte
werden	würde
wissen	wüsste

Four Modal verbs add an umlaut in the Imperfect Subjunctive:

Verb	Imperfect Subjunctive
dürfen	dürfte
können	könnte
mögen	möchte
müssen	müsste

The Perfect and Pluperfect Subjunctive are formed by using the Present or Imperfect Subjunctive of *haben* or *sein* + Past participle. There are no exceptions.

INDIRECT SPEECH

Direct speech > Indirect speech	Direct speech	Indirect speech
Present tense > Present Subjunctive unless same as Indicative, in which case use Imperfect Subjunctive	'Ich spiele im Kindergarten.' 'Wir gehen in die Stadt.'	Er sagte, er spiele im Kindergarten. Sie sagten, sie gingen in die Stadt.
Future tense > Conditional	'Ich werde es probieren.'	Sie sagte, sie würde es probieren.
Perfect or Pluperfect > Perfect Subjunctive unless same as Indicative, in which case use Pluperfect Subjunctive	'Ich habe es bestellt.' 'Wir haben es gesehen.'	Sie sagte, dass sie es bestellt habe. Sie sagten, dass sie es gesehen hätten.
Imperfect or Perfect > Pluperfect Subjunctive	'Wir gingen in die Stadt.'	Sie sagten, sie wären in die Stadt gegangen.

EXERCISES

P Put the following statements into Direct speech.

1 Sie sagte, sie habe es getrunken.

2 Wir sagten, es wäre zu spät, ins Restaurant zu gehen.

3 Sie hatte gesagt, dass Omeletts sehr schwer wären.

4 Ich habe gesagt, dass es leicht sei.

5 Sie sagte, dass sie es versuchen würde.

Q Now express these statements as indirect speech.

1 'Die Firma expandiert', sagte der Finanzleiter.

2 'Es wird schwierig sein', sagte mein Chef.

3 'Ich verstand die Lage nicht richtig', sagte er.

4 'Wir hatten zu viel in den Nahen Osten investiert', sagte er.

5 'Leider hatten wir zu viel verloren', sagte ich.

USES OF THE SUBJUNCTIVE

	Example	Meaning
It would be + Adjective.	Es wäre gut.	It would be good.
It would have been + Adjective.	Es wäre besser gewesen.	It would have been better.
als ob + Subjunctive	Sie handelten, als ob es problematisch wäre.	They acted as if it was problematic.

EXERCISE

R Revise 10.11. and then translate the following sentences into German.

1 It would be difficult.

2 It would have been more interesting.

3 If it had rained it would have been a catastrophe.

4 They acted as if it was difficult.

5 They would have recycled the paper if they had had time.

Particles, question tags and abbreviations

Contents

11.1 Particles

11.2 Question tags

11.3 Abbreviations

11.1 *Particles*

Particles are words used to indicate an attitude towards something, e.g. surprise or uncertainty. These nuances of feeling are often conveyed in English by intonation. It is hard to give exact definitions since the translation of particles can vary from phrase to phrase, from statement to question, command or exclamation, but the following guidelines should help.

Note that many of the particles, such as *aber*, *ja* and *vielleicht* have different meanings when not used as particles. (*Aber* = but, *ja* = yes, *vielleicht* = perhaps.)

Particles are not normally used at the start of a main clause before the main verb. Some can start a sentence if used as interjections. Contrast the use of *vielleicht* as 1. an adverb and 2. a particle:

1. *Vielleicht* ist es schwierig.   Perhaps it is difficult.

2. Das ist *vielleicht* schwierig.   That really is difficult.

Particle (and meaning when not used as a particle)	Usage as Particle	Example	Meaning
aber (but)	Expresses surprise	Das war *aber* ein interessanter Film!	That really was an interesting film!
allerdings/freilich	'Admittedly'	Die Musik war *allerdings/freilich* ziemlich schlecht.	The music was admittedly pretty bad.
also	'Thus' Used as an interjection meaning 'well'	Es ist *also* klar. *Also*, wir fangen hier an.	It is thus clear. Well, we are starting here.
auch (also)	Makes a w-question (*Wo*, *Was,* etc.) rhetorical	Was kann man *auch* machen?	What on earth can you do about it?
bloß (mere)	'Only' (less formal than *nur*)	Wenn Sie *bloß* mehr Zeit hätten!	If only you had more time!
denn (because)	Makes question less blunt	Wo ist er *denn*?	Where on earth is he?
doch	Interjection; positive response to negative question	Sind Sie nicht interessiert? *Doch*, ich bin sehr interessiert.	Are you not interested? Yes, I am very interested.
	Disagrees with a previous statement	Es ist *doch* ein Erfolg gewesen.	It has been a success after all.
	Speaker seeks agreement	Sie faxen es *doch* morgen, oder?	You are going to fax it tomorrow, aren't you?
	Used in commands to express impatience	Geben Sie mir *doch* endlich die Papiere!	For goodness sake, give me the papers.
	Used in commands to express encouragement	Versuchen Sie es *doch* morgen wieder!	Why don't you try again tomorrow?
eben	'Just', 'precisely'	Das ist *eben* das Problem.	That is precisely the problem.
eigentlich (real)	Makes a question more casual	Wo arbeiten Sie *eigentlich*?	Whereabouts do you actually work?
erst	'Only just'	Ihre Karriere hat *erst* begonnen.	Her career has only just begun.

Particle (and meaning when not used as a particle)	Usage as Particle	Example	Meaning
erst	Means 'only' or less than expected when used with quantities 'Not until' + time phrases 'Not before'+ time phrases	Sie ist *erst* 15. Sie hat *erst* 3 Seiten geschrieben. Wir fahren erst am Montag. Ich kann das Auto erst nächsten Monat reparieren.	She is only 15. She's only managed to write 3 pages. We're not going till Monday. I can't repair the car before next month.
etwa (approximately)	Implies something is undesirable	Wollen Sie *etwa* sagen, dass sie naiv ist?	Surely you're not trying to say that she is naive?
gar	Intensifies a negative	Ich habe *gar* nichts gesehen.	I have seen nothing at all.
immerhin	'Even so', 'all the same'	Es war *immerhin* ein guter Trickfilm.	Even so, it was was a good cartoon film.
ja (yes)	Used to stress the speaker is right Expresses surprise Implies a warning or threat	Das ist *ja* was ich sagte. Das ist *ja* unmöglich! Sie sollen *ja* nichts erzählen.	That is precisely what I was saying. That really is impossible. You should not say anything on any account.
jedenfalls	'At any rate', 'at least'	Der Film ist *jedenfalls* besser als die anderen.	At least the film is better than the others.
mal	Makes requests, commands and questions less blunt Combined with *doch* makes commands more casual	Geben Sie mir *mal* die Karten. Komm *doch mal* vorbei!	Give me the tickets please. Do come round some time!
noch (still)	Used to indicate more or further items	Ich möchte *noch* andere Regisseure kennenlernern.	I would like to get to know other film directors.
nun (now)	Used for emphasis, 'really'	Das ist *nun* schwer.	That really is difficult.
ruhig (quiet)	Used to reassure listener	Sie können *ruhig* länger bleiben.	You can gladly stay longer.

Particle (and meaning when not used as a particle)	Usage as Particle	Example	Meaning
schließlich (finally)	'After all'	Es ist *schließlich* Samstag.	It is Saturday, after all.
schon (already)	'Admittedly'	Das ist *schon* wahr, aber alte Filme sind besser.	That may admittedly be true, but old films are better.
	Used with nouns translates as 'The very ...'	*Schon* der Gedanke macht mich krank.	The very thought is enough to make me feel ill.
	Expresses confidence	Sie wird es *schon* schaffen.	I'm sure she'll manage it.
	Emphasises a condition	Wenn Sie *schon* exportieren, müssen sie vorsichtig sein.	If they are going to export they must be cautious.
sowieso	'In any case'	Jeder hat *sowieso* andere Ideen.	In any case everyone has different ideas.
überhaupt	Intensifies a negative word or concept	Es ist *überhaupt* problematisch.	However you look at it, it is problematic.
vielleicht (perhaps)	'Really'. Used in exclamations to express surprise	Das ist *vielleicht* dumm!	Well, that really is stupid!
wohl	Indicates something is fairly probable	Er ist *wohl* der neue Abteilungsleiter.	I expect he is the new Head of Department.
	Indicates speaker has reservations about something	Es ist *wohl* dramatisch, aber sehr unnatürlich.	It is indeed dramatic, but very unnatural.
zwar	'Admittedly'; usually followed by a clause with *aber* (but)	Sie haben *zwar* viel Positives gesagt, aber ich finde es trotzdem schlecht.	You have admittedly said a lot of positive things, but I still think it is bad.

The best way to get used to particles is to see how they are used. Listen and watch out for them!

EXERCISES

A Are *aber*, *ja* and *vielleicht* used as particles here or not?

1 Geht es Ihnen gut? *Ja.*

2 Ich war letzte Woche im Solarium, *aber* ich habe Sie nicht gesehen.

3 Wir waren *ja* auf Urlaub.

4 Das ist *aber* interessant.

5 *Vielleicht* können wir später Kaffee trinken.

6 Das ist *vielleicht* eine gute Idee.

7 *Ja*, ich habe wirklich Durst.

8 *Aber* ich habe nicht sehr viel Zeit.

B How do you translate each sentence? Insert the correct word.

1 I have only been here two days. Ich bin (allerdings/erst) zwei Tage hier.

2 So you haven't seen much yet? Sie haben (auch/also) nicht viel gesehen?

3 Yes, I have visited a lot of galleries. (Ja/Doch), ich habe viele Galerien besucht.

4 But, you've not seen much of the night-life, have you? Aber Sie haben (immerhin/gar) nicht viel vom Nachtleben gesehen, oder?

5 Tell me what there is to see then. Erzählen Sie (noch/mal), was es zu sehen gibt!

6 I'm quite happy to recommend some clubs, but I have never been to any. Ich kann Ihnen (vielleicht/ruhig) einige Clubs empfehlen, aber ich war nie drin.

7 After all, you are much older than I am. Sie sind (noch/schließlich) viel älter als ich.

8 In any case I am unfortunately too tired. Leider bin ich (sowieso/vielleicht) zu müde.

9 That really is a pity! Das ist (mal/vielleicht) schade!

10 I would like to go out, but it is too late. Ich würde (aber/zwar) gerne ausgehen, aber es ist zu spät.

11.2 *Question tags*

There are five main question tags in German. They are always preceded by a comma. They have no fixed meaning but correspond to the English 'isn't he', 'didn't it', 'haven't we', etc.

Question tag	Example	Meaning
gell? (used mainly in Austria and Bavaria)	Die Zwillinge wurden am Freitag getauft, *gell?*	The twins were baptised on Friday, weren't they?
ja?	Der Film beginnt um 8, *ja?*	The film begins at 8, doesn't it?
nicht wahr?	Du wirst deine Schwiegermutter besuchen, *nicht wahr?*	You are going to visit your mother-in-law, aren't you?

Question tag	Example	Meaning
nicht?	Deine Schwester hat den Film gesehen, *nicht?*	Your sister has seen the film, hasn't she?
oder?	Ihr Sohn fährt mit seiner Klasse nach Weimar, *oder?*	Your son is going with his class to Weimar, isn't he?
was? (mainly used for rhetorical questions)	Adoptiveltern haben es schwer, *was?*	It's difficult for adoptive parents, isn't it?

EXERCISE

C   Translate the following sentences into English.

  I   Meine Großtante hat am Sonntag Geburtstag, oder?

  2   Du hast schon die Adresse, nicht wahr?

  3   Ich habe dir die Einladung gegeben, nicht?

  4   Auf einer Party wird immer viel getrunken, was?

  5   Wir wollen eine Pfirsichbowle machen, gell?

  6   Du wirst Wein mitbringen, ja?

11.3 *Abbreviations*

There are obviously hundreds of abbreviations in common usage. Most relate to politics, business, culture, everyday life or aspects of a particular field (e.g. engineering). The following common abbreviations relate to language.

Abbreviation	Full form	Meaning
b.w.	bitte wenden	please turn over
bzw.	beziehungsweise	or rather/or indeed
d.h.	das heißt	that is to say
d.i.	das ist	that is
Forts. f.	Fortsetzung folgt	to be continued
S.	Seite	page
u.a.	unter anderem	among other things
u.dgl.	und dergleichen	and similar things
ü.d.M.	über dem Meeresspiegel	above sea-level
vgl.	vergleiche	compare
z.B.	zum Beispiel	for example
z.Zt.	zur Zeit	at the present time

EXERCISE

D Write the following sentences out in full.

1 Sie haben z.Zt. viele Pauschalreisen im Angebot.

2 D.h., sie haben natürlich auch Abenteuerreisen, aber sie sind teurer.

3 Sie können z.B. eine Safari-Reise machen.

4 Ein Urlaub auf dem Bauernhof bzw. auf dem Lande ist für Familien besonders attraktiv.

5 Es gibt u.a. ein Planetarium.

Key to exercises

I Basics

PAGE 4, EXERCISE A

1. Das Reisen ist immer interessant.

2. Ich fliege am Montag.

3. Wien ist die Hauptstadt von Österreich.

4. Es ist spät.

5. Gehen Sie bitte zur Passkontrolle.

6. Der Flughafen ist sehr groß.

7. Es gibt einen Flughafenbus.

8. Der Fahrer hat einen österreichischen Akzent.

PAGE 5, EXERCISE B

1. Milk.

2. Peppermint.

3. Apple.

4. Pancake.

5. Carrot.

6. Yoghurt.

7. Salt.

8. Lamb.

9. Coffee.

10. Vodka.

PAGE 6, EXERCISE C

1. intensity.

2. political.

3. statistics.

4. flexible.

5. harmonise.

6. university.

7. solidarity.

8. optimism.

9. tactics.

10. revolutionary.

PAGE 9, EXERCISE D

1. The restaurant was right by the lake.

2. There was a sculpture in the corner.

3. The waiter had a lot of spots.

4. The waitress was wearing a black skirt.

5. The guest was wearing a dinner-jacket.

6. How much money did the firm donate for the meal?

7. We have seen the new boss.

8. The waiter was carrying the glasses on a tray.

9. For breakfast there were rolls with jam and butter.

10. They sell crisps at the bar.

PAGE 10, EXERCISE E

1. Umweltpolitik (f) environmental policy.

2. Umweltministerium (nt) Ministry of the Environment.

3. Umweltfrage (f) environmental question/issue.

4. Umweltminister (m) Minister for the Environment.

5. Umweltstrategie (f) environmental strategy

PAGE 11, EXERCISE F

1. C zurückspringen = to jump back

2. F durchfahren = to drive through

3. I misshandeln = to maltreat, abuse

4. G zerreißen = to tear to pieces

5. A auslaufen = to run out (of supplies, etc.)

6. B niedergehen = to go down (of water level, etc.)

7. D losfahren = to set off

8. E vollfüllen = to fill up

9. J auseinanderfallen = to fall apart

10. H verschlafen = oversleep

PAGE 12, EXERCISE G

1. B die Schauspielerin = actress

2. D der Bonner = man from Bonn

3. A normalerweise = normally

4. E spielbar = playable

5. C Maler = painter

PAGE 12, EXERCISE H

1. Malerin

2. Hamburgerin

3. Schauspieler

4. netterweise; freundlicherweise

5. lesbar

2 Cases

PAGE 14, EXERCISE A

1. Wo ist **der** Dom?

2. Ich habe **den** Weihnachtsmarkt besucht.

3. Sie ist in **die** Stadt gegangen.

4. **Das** Rathaus liegt in der Altstadt.

5. Ich verbringe **den** Vormittag in der Stadtmitte.

6. Ohne **die** Fußgängerzone wäre die Stadt nicht so umweltfreundlich.

7. **Der** Bahnhof ist ganz modern.

8. Ich habe **den** Stadtpark gesehen.

9. Wir wandern durch **den** Thüringer Wald.

10. **Der** Nationalpark ist fantastisch.

PAGE 16, EXERCISE B

1. Trotz **des** Regens war es ein schöner Urlaub.

2. Sie kamen aus **der** Türkei.

3. Sie arbeitet bei **der** großen Reisefirma.

4. Das ist die Zentrale **der** Firma.

5. Wegen **des** Gewitters konnten wir nicht Wasserski fahren.

6. Sie gab **den** Touristen die Informationen.

7. Das Museum imponierte **den** Besuchern. (*imponieren* + Dat. See Chapter 10.)

8. Das Planetarium gehört **der** Stadt. (*gehören* + Dat. See Chapter 10.)

9. Das Fußballstadion war neben **dem** Sportzentrum.

10. Sie beschäftigten sich mit **der** Stadtgeschichte.

PAGE 17, EXERCISE C

1. Nominative. Subject of sentence.

2. Accusative. Direct object of verb *sehen*.

3. Dative. Indirect object of *geben*.

4. Genitive. Possession.

5. Accusative. Time phrase. Note there is no *s* added to the noun. The Genitive adjective ending for an adjective without any preceding determiner is *-en*.

6. Accusative. Time phrase.

7. Accusative. *Für* always takes Accusative.

8. Nominative. Verb *sein* always takes Nominative.

9. Accusative. *es gibt* + Accusative.

10. Dative. *Aus* always takes Dative.

11. Genitive. *Wegen* always takes Genitive.

12. Dative. *Von* always takes Dative.

13. Dative. Indirect object of *erklären*.

14. Accusative. Time phrase.

15. Genitive. Time phrase for regular events.

16. Genitive. 'of' in English.

17. Nominative. Verb *sein* always takes Nominative.

18. Accusative. *sprechen über* always takes Accusative (See Chapter 10.)

19. Accusative. Direct object.

20. Genitive. Time phrase.

3 Word order and conjunctions

PAGE 20, EXERCISE A

1. Die Galerie <u>besitzt</u> viele Bilder aus dem 19. Jahrhundert.

2. In dieser Galerie <u>sehen </u>wir viele Lithographien.

3. Offen gesagt, die Installationen <u>sind</u> nicht besonders interessant.

4. Weil die Bilder so schön sind, <u>müssen</u> sie hinter Glas sein.

5. Wie <u>finden</u> Sie dieses Stillleben?

6. Im Dritten Reich <u>wurden</u> viele Bilder <u>verboten</u>. (Passive. See Chapter 10.)

7. Übrigens, das Museum <u>ist</u> donnerstags bis 20.00 geöffnet.

8. Letztes Jahr <u>gab</u> es eine fantastische Kirchner-Ausstellung.

PAGE 21, EXERCISE B

1. Kurz, das Museum ist sehr interessant.

2. Offen gesagt, ich habe nicht viel Zeit.

3. Wie gesagt, ich muss die Ausstellung besuchen.

4. Mit anderen Worten, es ist nicht leicht.

5. Ehrlich gesagt, es ist unmöglich.

PAGE 21, EXERCISE C

1. Ist es sonnig in Rostock?

2. Hat es viel geregnet?

3. Kann es später windiger werden?

4. Gibt es viele Wolken?

5. War es ein Erfolg trotz des schlechten Wetters? *or* War es trotz des schlechten Wetters ein Erfolg?

PAGE 22, EXERCISE D

1. Nehmt die zweite Straße links.

2. Zeigen Sie mir den Stadtplan.

3. Warte vor dem Rathaus.

4. Parken wir hinter dem Supermarkt.

5. Bringen Sie mir die Karten.

PAGE 23, EXERCISE E

1. Ist es kalt, bleiben wir zu Hause.

2. Habe ich Zeit, lese ich die Zeitung.

3. Gehen Sie in die Disko, rufen Sie uns an.

4. Hat er Geld, kauft er CDs.

5. Haben Sie Zeit, hören Sie Volksmusik.

PAGE 23, EXERCISE F

1. Sie ist die Lehrerin, und sie ist sehr streng. *or* Sie ist die Lehrerin und ist sehr streng.

2. Die Region hat große Probleme mit Arbeitslosigkeit, aber es ist besonders schlimm auf dem Lande.

3. Er übersetzt Texte aus dem Deutschen ins Englische, oder er hilft seinen Kollegen.

4. Sie machten ein Praktikum in Deutschland, denn sie lernen da viel Deutsch.

5. Meine Kollegen arbeiten bis 6 Uhr, aber ich arbeite bis 4.

PAGE 25, EXERCISE G

1. Der Chef diktiert die Briefe, während die Sekretärin sie tippt.

2. Die Firma expandiert, weil das Produkt sehr erfolgreich ist.

3. Sie arbeiten den ganzen Nachmittag, obwohl sie sehr müde sind.

4. Die Filiale hat sehr viel Arbeit, zumal sie für die ganze Region verantwortlich ist.

5. Sie machten viele Überstunden, als ich in der Abteilung war.

6. Die Firma hatte ihren Hauptsitz in Bochum, bevor sie nach Stuttgart gezogen ist.

7. Sie haben die Firma umstrukturiert, damit sie mehr Profit machen.

8. Sie waren viel erfolgreicher, nachdem die Firma diversifiziert hatte.

9. Die Produkte sind sehr beliebt, obwohl sie sehr teuer sind.

10. Mehr Leute haben von der Firma gehört, seitdem sie mehr Fernsehspots machen.

PAGE 26, EXERCISE H

1. Ich habe gehört, Schindler hat vielen Menschen geholfen.

2. Man sagt, jemand hat einen Koffer mit Schindlers Liste gefunden.

3. Die Zeitung berichtet, der Koffer gehörte einer Frau in Hildesheim.

4. Sie sagen, Schindler ist jetzt krank.

5. Viele Leute sagen, der Film *Schindlers Liste* ist interessant.

6. Andere denken, der Film ist problematisch.

7. Einige behaupten, er ist zu melodramatisch.

8. Kritiker sagen, der Film stellt alles zu sentimental dar. (remember word order rules and separable prefixes – see Chapter 3.)

PAGE 27, EXERCISE I

1. Er steht um 8 auf.

2. Er geht zum Sportzentrum zurück.

3. Unsere Freunde sind um 4 zurückgekommen. *or* Unsere Freunde kamen um 4 zurück.

4. Das ist die Frau, die gestern angekommen ist. *or* Das ist die Frau, die gestern ankam.

5. Sie gaben DM200 im Sportgeschäft aus. *or* Sie haben DM200 im Sportgeschäft ausgegeben.

PAGE 27, EXERCISE J

1. Sie ist die Frau, die viel Bier trinkt.

2. Das ist der Koch, der gute Salate macht.

3. Das ist die Pizzeria, in der ich arbeitete.

4. Wo ist die Kellnerin, die uns alle bediente?

5. Ich dachte an das Wirtshaus, das gute Fischgerichte macht.

PAGE 28, EXERCISE K

1. Sie möchte die Speisekarte sehen. (*Sie will* sounds too forceful here.)

2. Ich möchte die Weinliste sehen.

3. Sie müssen mit Kreditkarte bezahlen.

4. Ich kann das Restaurant empfehlen.

5. Wir werden um 3.30 zum Café gehen.

6. Ich lasse ein Taxi bestellen.

7. Das Café ist schön, weil man da/dort Zeitungen lesen kann.

8. Es ist schön, weil wir einen Tisch haben reservieren können.

PAGE 29, EXERCISE L

1. Wann haben Sie Geburtstag?

2. Sie setzten ihn unter Druck.

3. Ich weiß, wann er Geburtstag hat.

4. Sie sagten, dass sie viele Videos zur Verfügung haben.

5. Sie haben heute Glück gehabt.

PAGE 30, EXERCISE M

1. Ich habe Drogen nicht genommen. (If you said 'Ich habe nicht Drogen genommen.' this would mean that you took something else instead. The listener would be waiting to hear the 'sondern', followed by what was taken, e.g. 'Ich habe nicht Drogen genommen, sondern Antiobiotika.')

2. Sie hat nie sehr viel geraucht.

3. Er hat die Drogenprobleme nicht richtig analysiert.

4. Die Frau hat nie Heroin genommen.

5. Sie ist nicht zur Drogenberatungsstelle gegangen.

6. Viele haben nicht ganz aufgehört, Drogen zu nehmen.

PAGE 30, EXERCISE N

1. Sie fährt am Montag nach Genf. (Genf = Geneva)

2. Er fliegt am Donnerstag mit British Airways.

3. Wir wandern den ganzen Tag in den Alpen.

4. Meine Kusine kommt mit dem Taxi vom Bahnhof.

5. Sie reist zu Weihnachten mit der Bahn nach Italien. *or* Zu Weihnachten reist sie mit der Bahn nach Italien. The latter sounds much better because it avoids three adverbial phrases together.

PAGE 31, EXERCISE O

1. Wir schickten ihnen die Blumen.

2. Ich gab sie meiner Mutter.

3. Sie gab ihrem Mann das Buch.

4. Er lieh es seinem Freund. *or* Er lieh es seiner Freundin. (If the 'it' refers to a Masc. noun – 'Er lieh ihn seinem Freund', and if 'it' refers to a Fem. noun, 'Er lieh sie seinem Freund.')

5. Sie gab ihm das Buch zurück.

6. Ich schickte es ihnen. *or* Ich schickte ihn ihnen. *or* Ich schickte sie ihnen.

7. Sie zeigten ihm das Buch.

8. Er zeigte ihnen die Pläne.

9. Sie gaben dem Manager die Uhr.

10. Wir verkauften unseren Freunden das Auto.

PAGE 32, EXERCISE P

1. No. No noun preceded by a preposition can be the subject.

2. Yes.

3. No. She is the Direct Object and Accusative.

4. No. *Für* always takes the Accusative.

5. No. The verb is plural and *Studentin* is singular, so this should set alarm bells ringing. She is the Direct Object and Accusative. The subject is *sie*.

PAGE 33, EXERCISE Q

1. Den Managern haben <u>sie</u> die Informationen gegeben.

2. Mit den Maschinen hatten <u>sie</u> immer Probleme.

3. Die Abteilungsleiterin fanden <u>sie</u> alle sehr sympathisch.

4. <u>Es</u> ist relativ leicht, die Probleme zu verstehen.

5. Den Journalisten haben <u>sie</u> interessant gefunden.

6. Aus vielen Gründen kann <u>das Projekt</u> problematisch werden.

7. Gegenüber vom Eingang steht <u>der Leiter</u> des Büros.

8. Nach den letzten Tagen kann <u>man</u> nicht mehr von einem guten Manager sprechen.

9. Einen Monat lang kam <u>keine Nachricht</u> von ihr.

10. Trotz der Schwierigkeiten haben <u>sie</u> es gut gemacht.

4 *Numbers and Statistics*

PAGE 36, EXERCISE A

1. zwölf

2. vierzig

3. zehn

4. fünfundfünfzig

5. siebzehn

PAGE 37, EXERCISE B

1. Mein Büro ist im fünften Stock.

2. Es ist das zweitbeste Ergebnis dieses Jahr.

3. Die Messe beginnt am dritten Januar. *or* Die Messe beginnt am 3. Januar.

4. Der Film ist über Werbung im 20. Jahrhundert.

PAGE 38, EXERCISE C

1. Es gibt **zweierlei** Regionen.

2. Sie investierten **dreimal** so viel in die Infrastruktur.

3. Sie sind jetzt **sechsmal** attraktiver als vorher.

4. **Ende der neunziger Jahre** mussten viele Arbeiter neue Stellen finden. *or* **Ende der 90er Jahre** mussten viele Arbeiter neue Stellen finden.

5. **Ein Dutzend** Städte arbeiten eng zusammen.

6. **Mitte der 90er** exportierte die Firma viel nach Frankreich. *or* **Mitte der neunziger Jahre** exportierte die Firma viel nach Frankreich.

PAGE 39, EXERCISE D

1. Die Pressekonferenz ist am einundzwanzigsten April. *or* Die Pressekonferenz ist am 21. April.

2. Die Demonstration ist am Mittwochnachmittag.

3. Die Wahl ist am Donnerstag, den 14. Februar.

4. Die Debatte ist um Mittag.

5. Die Russische Revolution war Anfang des zwanzigsten Jahrhunderts. *or* Die Russische Revolution war Anfang des 20. Jahrhunderts.

PAGE 40, EXERCISE E

1. zu Ostern/am Ostermontag

2. zu Weihnachten/zu Ostern

3. zu Sylvester (fireworks are a New Year tradition in Germany)

4. am Aschermittwoch

5. am Tag der Einheit/am 3.10.

PAGES 41–2, EXERCISE F

1. im Jahre 1989 *or* 1989 (in 1989 is also gradually creeping into general use)

2. erst um Mitternacht

3. bis vor kurzem

4. Anfang Oktober

5. Ende Januar

6. im Herbst

7. Tag für Tag

8. Es war am Mittwoch, den 30. Januar.

9. auf die Dauer

10. am Samstagnachmittag

11. halb acht/sieben Uhr dreißig

12. im Winter

13. in den 20er Jahren

14. zweiundzwanzig Uhr fünfundfünfzig

15. in letzter Zeit; neulich

16. Es gibt einen Dom, und es gibt vier Museen (*or* Es gibt einen Dom und vier Museen.)

17. Es gibt Hunderte von Kneipen.

18. Es gibt Dutzende von Cafés.

19. Es gibt Millionen.

20. Ich habe am 29. (neunundzwanzigsten) Juni Geburtstag.

PAGE 42, EXERCISE G

1. Ich möchte einen Beutel Chips.

2. Ich möchte eine Dose Tomaten.

3. Ich möchte einen Liter Wein.

4. Ich möchte ein halbes Pfund Kirschen.

5. Ich möchte ein Glas Marmelade.

1. Die Temperatur stieg um 2%. *or* Die Temperatur ist um 2% gestiegen.

2. Die Hälfte der Leute in der Region leidet unter den Emissionen. (NB singular verb see Chapter 10.)

3. Zwei Drittel der Leute nehmen ihre Flaschen zum Altglascontainer.

4. Die Umweltverschmutzung in dieser Region ist um 2% gesunken.

5. 72,5% fahren mit dem Auto zur Arbeit. (NOTE the comma!)

5 *Nouns*

1. Wo ist **das** Zentrum?

2. **Das** Museum ist neben dem Dom.

3. **Die** Bücherei ist in der Stadtmitte.

4. **Die** Lehrerin arbeitet in der Stadt.

5. Wo ist **die** Universität?

1. Elefant Masc. animal

2. Europa Neut. continent

3. Frankreich Neut. country

4. Gold Neut. metal

5. Lamm Neut. young animal

6. Nebel Masc. weather

7. Oktober Masc. month

8. Rhein Masc. river

9. Süden Masc. point of compass

10. Tante Fem. female person

PAGE 49, EXERCISE C

1. For many the Brandenburg Gate is the symbol of Berlin.

2. The wise man knows everything about the history of Berlin.

3. The leader of the group comes from a suburb of Berlin.

4. Where can you play golf in Berlin?

5. You find a lot of flowers on the heath that you don't see in Berlin.

PAGE 49, EXERCISE D

1. Atomenergie Fem. *-ie* is a Fem. ending

2. Bundesministerium Neut. *-um* is a Neut. ending.

3. Innenminister Masc. *-er* is normally a Masc. ending. It refers to a male person.

4. Politiklehrerin Fem. *-in* is a Fem. ending

5. Friedenspolitik Fem. *-ik* is a Fem. ending.

PAGE 50, EXERCISE E

1. Die Brille **liegt** auf dem Tisch.

2. Lebensmittel **sind** hier sehr teuer.

3. Die Möbel **sind** alle aus Schweden.

4. Ihre Hose **sieht** sehr elegant **aus**.

5. Die Zinsen **sind** leider sehr hoch.

6. Die Wahl **findet** am Montag **statt**.

PAGES 52–3, EXERCISE F

1. Die **Ateliers liegen** in der Stadtmitte.

2. Die **Interessen** der Gruppe **sind** an der EU.

3. Die **Risiken sind** groß.

4. Die **Chefs fliegen** oft in die USA.

5. Die **Computer sind** 4 Jahre alt.

6. Die **Erfolge** der Projekte **sind** klar.

7. Die **Häfen sind** international bekannt.

8. Die **Männer arbeiten** bei einer Software-Firma.

9. Die **Namen waren** weltbekannt.

10. Die **Streiks haben** nicht lange gedauert.

11. Die **Firmen haben** ihren Hauptsitz in Bayern.

12. Die **Städte sind** multikulturell.

PAGE 54, EXERCISE G

1. Am Anfang des **Jahres** kamen viele Asylsuchende nach Deutschland.

2. Nach einigen **Jahren** haben sie sich in der Stadt etabliert.

3. Für den **Optimisten** ist das Leben in einem neuen Land immer schön.

4. Jeder will einen netten **Nachbarn** haben.

5. Die Zahl der **Arbeitslosen** ist in letzter Zeit gestiegen.

PAGE 55, EXERCISE H

1. Für viele **Erwachsene** ist Weihnachten weniger interessant.

2. Meine **Bekannten** feiern am 1. Weihnachtstag.

3. Bei vielen **Arbeitslosen** spielt Alkohol eine Rolle.

4. Einige **Deutsche** fahren dreimal im Jahr auf Urlaub.

5. Die Hauptprobleme der **Obdachlosen** haben mit der Gesundheit zu tun.

PAGE 56, EXERCISE I

1. Er ging mit seinen Kollegen, den Lehrern, zur Demonstration.

2. Er lebte in einer 2-Zimmer-Wohnung, einer Wohnung am Stadtrande.

3. Wir kauften Möbel für meinen Untermieter, einen Studenten.

4. Das ist die Hauptindustrie in Schwerin, der Hauptstadt des Landes Mecklenburg-Vorpommern.

6 *Articles*

PAGES 58–9, EXERCISE A

1. Der Arzt kommt aus der Tschechischen Republik. (Use *von* for journeys from, *aus* for originating from a place. See Chapter 9.)

2. Er wohnt in der Bahnhofstraße.

3. Er ging in die Stadt.

4. Er fuhr mit dem Bus nach Köln.

5. Er brach sich das Bein.

6. Sein Bruder lebt in den USA. (NB plural country – USA)

7. Er kommt im Frühling nach Deutschland.

8. Seine Schwester lebt seit April in Aachen. (Present tense + *seit* – See Chapter 10.)

9. Ihre Operation ist am Mittwoch. *or* Sie wird am Mittwoch operiert.

10. Trauben kosten DM4 das Pfund.

PAGE 59, EXERCISE B

1. Heute hat **eine** Frau mehr Möglichkeiten als vor 100 Jahren.

2. Auch wenn sie **eine** Familie hat, kann sie weiterarbeiten.

3. Eine Frau mit **einer** guten Stelle kann viel verdienen.

4. In einer idealen Welt gibt es **keine** Diskriminierung.

5. Es gibt **keinen** Grund, Frauen weniger Geld für die gleiche Arbeit zu geben.

PAGE 60, EXERCISE C

1. Ich habe Kopfschmerzen. *or* Mir tut der Kopf weh.

2. Das war Geschmackssache.

3. Die Arbeit endet um Viertel vor fünf. *or* Die Arbeit ist um Viertel vor fünf aus.

4. Ich arbeite als Krankenschwester.

5. Sie ist Zahnärztin.

6. Es ist zu Ende.

7. Sie spricht als Ärztin.

8. Sie ist eine gute Ärztin.

PAGE 61, EXERCISE D

1. **Dieses** Wetter ist ungewöhnlich gut.

2. **Dieser** Wind ist sehr stark.

3. **Diese** Temperaturen sind nicht typisch.

4. Bei **dieser** Sonne wird man schnell braun.

5. Aus **diesem** Grund ist das Klima hier besser als im Gebirge.

PAGES 61–2, EXERCISE E

1. **Beide** Gruppen sind aus Hamburg.

2. Wir arbeiten mit **beiden** Gruppen zusammen.

3. **Jede** ethnische Gruppe ist anders.

4. **Welche** Vorteile hat das Leben in einer Großstadt?

5. **Einige** Leute wohnen lieber auf dem Lande.

PAGE 62, EXERCISE F

1. He is the same man who was playing in the concert yesterday.

2. The girl who wants to play tennis can go now.

3. Anyone who likes playing golf will find wonderful golf courses here.

4. For those who like swimming there is an open-air pool.

7 *Pronouns*

PAGE 64, EXERCISE A

1. **Du** nimmst 3 Zwiebeln.

2. **Ich** nehme 250g Tomaten.

3. **Wir** backen eine Pizza.

4. **Man** muss die Pizza 25 Minuten backen.

5. Meine Brüder kommen uns besuchen. **Sie** essen sehr gerne Pizza.

6. Meine Mutter macht sie oft für **uns**.

7. Ich helfe **ihr** manchmal. (*helfen* + Dat. See Chapter 10.)

8. Vater hilft ungern. Ich sehe **ihn** ganz selten in der Küche.

PAGE 65, EXERCISE B

1. Ich wasche **mir** die Haare.

2. Er wäscht **sich**.

3. Du erinnerst **dich**.

4. Wir setzen **uns** hier hin.

5. Sie interessieren **sich** für Kunst.

PAGE 66, EXERCISE C

1. Das Hotel befindet sich in Rostock. *or* Das Hotel ist in Rostock. The former is more formal.

2. Mein Bruder hat sich dort erkältet.

3. Jetzt hat er sich erholt.

4. Er entschloss sich, nach Magdeburg zu fahren.

5. Wir verabschiedeten uns von ihm.

PAGE 67, EXERCISE D

1. Sie ist die Frau, **die** in Berlin arbeitet.

2. Sie ist die Frau, **deren** Firma erfolgreich ist.

3. Hier ist der Mann, mit **dem** ich arbeite.

4. Sie sind die Leute, **deren** Computer neu sind.

PAGES 67–8, EXERCISE E

1. Wo ist das Buch, **das** ich kaufte?

2. Ich sah den Computer, **den** Sie kauften.

3. Das ist die Firma, **deren** Produkte so gut sind.

4. Das ist das Gebäude, in **dem** wir arbeiten.

5. Haben Sie die Maschine gesehen, **die** wir gemacht/gedreht haben?

6. Ich mag die Produkte, **die** Sie beschrieben. *or* Mir gefallen die Produkte, **die** Sie beschrieben.

7. Wo sind die Manager, **deren** Produkte so schlecht waren?

8. Er ist der Mann, **dessen** Firma in Berlin ist.

9. Sie ist die Frau, **der** ich die Bücher verkauft habe.

10. Das ist das Produkt, **das** ich mag. *or* Das ist das Produkt, **das** mir gefällt.

PAGE 68, EXERCISE F

1. Wer ist der Manager?

2. Wen haben Sie gesehen? *or* Wen hast du gesehen? *or* Wen habt ihr gesehen?

3. Wessen Produkte haben Sie gekauft?

4. Für wen reservierten Sie es? *or* Für wen haben Sie es reserviert?

5. Mit wem gingen Sie? *or* Mit wem sind Sie gegangen?

6. Wessen Fabrik ist das?

7. Was ist das?

8. Wem haben Sie geholfen? (*helfen* + Dat. See Chapter 10.)

PAGES 69–70, EXERCISE G

1. Wofür interessiert sie sich?

2. Worauf wartet die Firma?

3. Worin sehen Sie das Problem?

4. Wovon sprechen Sie? *or* Worüber sprechen Sie?

5. Ich weiß nicht, worauf sie wartet.

6. Ich weiß, wofür sie sich interessieren.

PAGE 70, EXERCISE H

1. Das ist nicht mein Problem. Es ist **deins**.

2. Haben Sie Ihre Karte? Ich habe **meine**.

3. Ich habe meine Probleme diskutiert. Sie diskutierte **ihre**.

4. Ich machte es trotz meiner Probleme. Sie machte es trotz **ihrer**.

5. Ich kaufe eine Kassette für meine Mutter. Du kaufst eine Kassette für **deine**.

6. Er nahm sein Auto. Ich nahm **meins**.

7. Das erste Konzert ist in meiner Stadt. Das zweite Konzert ist in **Ihrer**.

8. Wo sind die Büros? **Meins** ist im ersten Stock.

9. Ich sah meine Freundin. Paul sah **seine**.

10. Wir kauften unsere Fahrkarten. Sie kauften **ihre**.

PAGE 72, EXERCISE I

1. Niemand versteht es.

2. Alles ist klar.

3. Etwas ist kaputt.

4. Nichts ist hier/da. (The Germans sometimes use *da* where English use 'here'.)

5. Ein bisschen bleibt.

PAGE 72, EXERCISE J

1. Beide haben viel Geld.

2. Einige hatten keine Wohnung.

3. Mehrere hatten Probleme.

4. Manche/einige hatten Schwierigkeiten mit Wohnungen.

8 *Adjectives and adverbs*

PAGE 74, EXERCISE A

1. Die **Leipziger** Messe hat eine lange Tradition.

2. **Ganz** Deutschland litt unter den Folgen des Krieges.

3. In den **achtziger** Jahren protestierten viele DDR-Bürger gegen das Regime.

4. Es war **wirklich** warm in Halle.

5. Die **ganze** Ostseeküste ist sehr beliebt bei Touristen.

6. Vom Standpunkt der Literaturgeschichte ist Weimar besonders **interessant**.

PAGE 76, EXERCISE B

1. Sie fahren durch eine **kleine** Stadt.

2. Für **englische** Touristen gibt es Prospekte auf Deutsch und Englisch.

3. Jeder **neue** Gast kann sich in das Gästebuch eintragen.

4. Mein **alter** Reiseführer ist nicht mehr sehr nützlich.

5. Fünf **zentrale** Hotels existieren nicht mehr.

6. Einige **historische** Sehenswürdigkeiten sind noch geöffnet.

7. Es gibt **vietnamesische** Restaurants in der Nähe des Marktplatzes.

8. Sie haben den **alten** Bahnhof restauriert.

PAGE 76, EXERCISE C

1. Das ist ein **teures** Produkt.

2. Das ist eine **flexible** Lösung.

3. Das ist eine sehr **hohe** Inflationsrate.

4. Leider ist das die **bittre** Wahrheit.

PAGES 78–9, EXERCISE D

1. Im Norden ist es windiger **als** im Süden.

2. In Erfurt ist es genauso warm **wie** in Magdeburg.

3. In Kiel ist es am **kältesten**.

4. München ist mit 20 Grad die **wärmste** Stadt Deutschlands.

5. Gestern war es im Südwesten **länger** sonnig.

6. Im Osten wird der Wind am **schwächsten** sein.

7. In Nürnberg war die Temperatur **höher** als in Erfurt.

8. In Saarbrücken hat es gestern am **meisten** geregnet.

PAGE 79, EXERCISE E

1. Dies/Das ist mein Gymnasium.

2. Frau Nause ist meine neue Lehrerin.

3. Ich arbeite mit Anna, meiner Klassenkameradin. (Noun in apposition. See Chapter 5.)

4. Ihr Lieblingsfach ist Kunst.

5. Unsere nächsten Prüfungen sind im Juli.

PAGE 80, EXERCISE F

1. **Diese** Region ist sehr flach.

2. **Welcher** Fluss fließt durch Frankfurt?

3. Sind **jene** Berge im Süden Deutschlands?

4. In **jedem** Naturpark kann man wunderschön wandern.

5. An **welcher** Küste liegt Bremerhaven?

PAGE 81, EXERCISE G

1. Ich bin es **satt**, im Zug schlecht zu essen.

2. Es ist mir **egal**, ob es teuer ist.

3. Es ist mir einfach **lästig**, Reiseproviant mitzuschleppen.

4. Eigentlich ist es mir **unbegreiflich**, warum sie nichts Leckeres servieren.

5. Den Kellnern muss es oft **peinlich** sein, wenn das Essen so miserabel ist.

6. Meiner Mutter bin ich **dankbar**, wenn sie mir ein Lunchpaket mitgibt.

PAGE 83, EXERCISE H

1. Er ist vorbereitet **auf** die Expansion der Firma.

2. Der Preis ist unabhängig **von** der Inflationsrate.

3. Das ist typisch **für** unsere Produkte.

4. Der Marketing-Manager ist sehr empfänglich **für** neue Impulse.

5. Die Praktikantin war sehr dankbar **für** die Hilfe.

6. Sie sind **mit** den Kunden einverstanden.

7. Viele sind gleichgültig **gegenüber** den Innovationen.

8. Sie sind überzeugt **von** der Richtigkeit der neuen Pläne.

9. Die Abteilungsleiterin ist einverstanden **mit** den Plänen.

10. Sie ist **für** Werbung zuständig.

11. Der Finanzmanager ist **an** Computern interessiert.

12. Sie sind sehr stolz **auf** die Exporte.

13. Er ist begeistert **von** dem neuen Modell.

14. Das Produkt ist reich **an** Kalorien.

15. Das ist geeignet **für** das Ausland.

PAGE 84, EXERCISE I

1. **Heute** gibt es viele karitative Organisationen in Deutschland.

2. **Überall** gibt es interessante lokale Projekte.

3. **Natürlich/Selbstverständlich** versuchen einige Gruppen, auch international aktiv zu sein.

4. Sie helfen **dort**, wo sie gebraucht werden.

5. Sie freuen sich **immer**, Spenden zu bekommen.

6. **Manchmal** haben sie nicht immer genug Geld, um viel machen zu können.

7. Sie kooperieren **trotzdem** mit internationalen Organisationen.

8. **Sonst** fühlen sie sich manchmal sehr isoliert.

PAGE 85, EXERCISE J

1. **Wann** fahren Sie nach Deutschland?

2. **Wie lange** bleiben Sie dort?

3. **Wo** wohnen Sie im Moment?

4. **Warum** arbeiten Sie in Bremen?

5. **Wohin** fahren Sie zu Weihnachten?

9 *Prepositions*

PAGE 88, EXERCISE A

1. Ich kaufte es **für** meine Mutter.

2. Sie machte es **wider** meinen Willen.

3. Sie ging **durch** den Wald, weil es da so schön war.

4. Sie joggte dann viermal **um** den Block.

5. **Ohne** einen Regenschirm werden Sie nass werden.

6. Sie nehmen Tabletten **gegen** Kopfschmerzen.

7. Ich fuhr mit meiner Familie den Rhein **entlang**.

8. Meine Oma bezahlte viel **pro** Quadratmeter für ihre Wohnung.

9. Mein Mann und ich spielten **gegen** meine Schwiegereltern.

10. Er schickte eine Geburtstagskarte **per** e-mail.

PAGE 89, EXERCISE B

1. Er sucht **nach** seinem Regenschirm.

2. Ich sehne mich **nach** der Sonne.

3. Die Salbe ist **gegen** Sonnenbrand.

4. Wir bekamen Handschuhe **zu** Weihnachten.

5. Wir fahren für drei Monate **zum** Nordpol.

6. Er wohnt seit zwei Monaten **im** Regenwald.

PAGES 90–1, EXERCISE C

1. Sie ist **zu** ihrer Schwester nach Polen gefahren.

2. Sie ist Engländerin, aber er kommt **aus** Schottland.

3. Er lebt **seit** drei Jahren in den USA.

4. Das Reisebüro ist **gegenüber** dem Bahnhof.

5. Sie haben ihre Koffer **bei** C & A gekauft.

6. **Nach** dem Urlaub in Spanien ist es schwer, wieder ins Büro zu gehen.

7. Bern ist die Hauptstadt **von** der Schweiz.

8. Weil er so oft auf Geschäftsreisen ist, ist er nicht oft **zu** Hause.

9. Wir flogen **von** Düsseldorf nach Wien.

10. Sie arbeitete zehn Jahre **bei** Mercedes.

PAGE 92, EXERCISE D

1. Ich war in **der** Stadtmitte.

2. Sie ging in **die** Bäckerei.

3. Wir spielten hinter **dem** Supermarkt.

4. Der Weihnachtsmarkt war vor **dem** Rathaus.

5. Das Museum ist zwischen dem Dom und **dem** Bahnhof.

6. Sie ging in **die** Galerie.

7. Wir treffen uns in **der** Eisdiele.

PAGE 93, EXERCISE E

1. Unter anderem sind Drogen teuer.

2. Unter uns, ich glaube, sie ist krank.

3. Der Boxer wohnt im ersten Stock.

4. Die Sendung über Drogen war im Fernsehen.

5. Wir sprachen unter vier Augen über ihre Krankheit.

PAGE 94, EXERCISE F

1. Sie fliegt **nach** Dresden.

2. Sie geht **zum** Bahnhof.

3. Ich fahre **in die** Stadt.

4. Wir fahren **zu** meinem Bruder. (**zu** = to the house of)

5. Meine Schwester fährt **ans** Meer.

6. Ich gehe heute **ins** Kino.

7. Er geht **auf** die Toilette.

8. Sie fliegt **in** die USA. (die USA = plural country)

PAGE 94, EXERCISE G

1. Der Supermarkt ist in der Stadtmitte.

2. Er geht ins Kaufhaus.

3. Sie sind in der Galerie.

4. Er ging ins Kino.

5. Es ist zwischen der Apotheke und dem Café.

PAGE 95, EXERCISE H

1. **Trotz** des schlechten Wetters gingen sie schwimmen.

2. **Während** der Mittagspause haben sie eingekauft.

3. **Wegen** des Schnees war es nicht möglich, nach Italien zu fahren.

4. **Unterhalb** der Schneegrenze konnte man eine Wanderung machen.

5. **Oberhalb** der Schneegrenze konnte man Ski fahren.

10 *Verbs*

PAGE 98, EXERCISE A

1. expandieren – yes

2. tun – yes

3. immun – no, it's an adjective

4. investieren – yes

5. innovativ – no, it's an adjective

6. handeln – yes

7. sein – yes

8. verkaufen – yes

PAGES 100–1, EXERCISE B

1. ändern – weak

2. essen – strong

3. gehen – strong

4. angeln – weak

5. analysieren – weak

6. adaptieren – weak

7. trinken – strong

8. verlieren – strong

9. wandern – weak

10. parken – weak

PAGE 102, EXERCISE C

1. Ich **besuche** das Schloss mit meiner Kusine.

2. Du **bezahlst** die Karten für das Konzert.

3. Die Dame **zeigt** den Besuchern den Eingang.

4. Wir **diskutieren** die Geschichte des Schlosses.

5. Die Touristen **warten** auf die Führung.

PAGE 102, EXERCISE D

1. Er **findet** Mathe schwer.

2. Frau Braun **schließt** die Klassenzimmertür sehr laut.

3. Paul **antwortet** nicht sehr oft.

4. Die Lehrerin **klingelt** an der Tür.

5. Du **faxt** die Informationen über den Austausch.

PAGES 103–4, EXERCISE E

1. Die Assistentin **hilft** mit den Deutschstunden.

2. Er **läuft** schneller als die anderen Jungs in seiner Klasse.

3. Frau Tschärtner **spricht** Polnisch, Deutsch und Englisch.

4. Wir **lesen** einen Roman von Christa Wolf.

5. Die Geschichtslehrerin **empfiehlt** den neuen Film über den Holocaust.

6. Paula **nimmt** ihr Studium sehr ernst.

7. Die Klasse **fährt** dieses Jahr nach Berlin.

8. Mittags **esse** ich immer in der Schulkantine.

9. Die Straßenbahn **hält** direkt vor dem Gymnasium.

10. Meine Freundin **gibt** mir das Handout.

PAGE 105, EXERCISE F

1. Ich **bin** in derselben Partei wie meine Mutter.

2. Er **lässt** die Besucher allein.

3. Wir **sind** schon sehr lange Mitglieder der SPD.

4. Seine Ideen **haben** viel Einfluss auf den Kanzler.

5. Ich **weiß**, dass sie sich für Politik interessieren.

6. Niemand **hat** viel von seinen Plänen gehört.

7. Im Winter **wird** es in Berlin kälter als in Bonn.

8. Er **tut** sein Bestes für seine Partei.

9. Ihr **seid** die jüngsten Mitglieder der Partei.

10. Der Präsident **weiß**, dass es schwer sein wird.

PAGES 105–6, EXERCISE G

1. Ich **muss** viel Obst essen.

2. Man **darf** hier nicht rauchen.

3. Es **kann** schwer sein, fit zu bleiben.

4. Du **sollst** jeden Morgen joggen.

5. Meine Kusine **mag** Pommes und Pralinen, aber sie versucht abzunehmen.

6. Er **will** jeden Tag zum Sportzentrum gehen.

PAGES 106–7, EXERCISE H

1. Gehen Sie links!

2. Kommen Sie herein!

3. Kommen Sie später zurück!

4. Gehen wir zum Rathaus zurück!

5. Gehen wir in die Stadt!

6. Gib mir die Karten!

7. Zeigen Sie mir Ihren Pass!

8. Steigen Sie in den Bus ein!

PAGE 107, EXERCISE I

1. Bedienung!

2. Ruhe!

3. Volltanken!

4. Achtung!

5. Verzeihung! *or* Entschuldigung!

PAGE 108, EXERCISE J

1. Ich werde in die Schweiz fahren.

2. Sie wird eine Karte kaufen.

3. Sie werden in den Alpen Ski fahren.

4. Sie werden ein schweizerisches Stück sehen.

5. Wir werden die Schweiz studieren.

PAGE 109, EXERCISE K

1. Become

2. Future

3. Become (Imperfect tense)

4. Future

5. Passive

6. Become

7. Passive

8. Future

9. Passive

10. Future

PAGE 110, EXERCISE L

1. Der Regisseur **drehte** einen neuen Film.

2. Sie **studierte** viele deutsche Filme.

3. Ein Journalist **fotografierte** die Filmstars.

4. Sie **kritisierte** den Fassbinder-Film.

5. Wir **parkten** vor dem Filmstudio in Babelsberg.

6. Meine Freundin **spielte** Klarinette.

7. Ihr **kauftet** eine Videokassette.

8. Er **arbeitete** als Stuntman.

PAGE 111, EXERCISE M

1. Er **griff** sofort zu Aspirin.

2. Er **blieb** eine Woche im Bett.

3. Die Mutter **schrieb** eine Geschichte über ein Krankenhaus.

4. Sie **litt** an Asthma.

5. Sie **schnitt** sich am Arm.

6. Der Arzt **stieg** in sein Auto ein.

PAGE 112, EXERCISE N

1. Sein Koffer **wog** 20 Kilos.

2. Man **schloss** die Tür des Flugzeugs.

3. Er **flog** nach München.

4. Die Stewardess **bot** ein Getränk und einen Imbiss.

5. Er **verlor** seine Flugtickets.

6. Die Touristen **froren**.

PAGE 112, EXERCISE O

1. Ich **fand** die Lebkuchen lecker.

2. Er **zwang** mich, zum Weihnachtsmarkt zu gehen.

3. Am Marktplatz **begann** die Gruppe, Lieder zu singen.

4. Wir **tranken** viel Glühwein.

5. Ich **gewann** einen Fisch.

6. Der Fisch **schwamm** in einem Glas.

7. Sie **empfahl** den Sekt.

8. Ich **nahm** ein Glas Pfirsichbowle.

9. Wir **trafen** uns vor der Konzerthalle.

10. Sie **sprachen** über die wunderbaren Feuerwerke.

PAGE 112, EXERCISE P

1. Was **geschah** in der Imbissstube?

2. Ich **aß** Pizza mit Champignons.

3. Er **gab** mir das Rezept.

4. Er **vergaß** seinen Termin im Wirtshaus.

5. Sie **saß** im Lokal.

PAGE 112, EXERCISE Q

1. Die Gewinne **wuchsen** schnell.

2. Der Marketing-Manager **fuhr** nach Frankfurt.

3. Wir **hielten** die Konferenz in dem Messezentrum.

4. Ich **ließ** meine Dokumente im Büro.

5. Wir **rieten** Ihnen, die Aktien zu verkaufen.

PAGE 113, EXERCISE R

1. Die Museumsdirektorin **sandte** mir ein paar Prospekte.

2. Das war schön, weil ich die Stadt gar nicht **kannte**.

3. Mein Freund **nannte** ein paar Sehenswürdigkeiten, die ich besuchen könnte.

4. Ich **dachte**, dass das neue Museum vielleicht von Interesse ist.

5. Ich **wusste** nicht, wie viel der Eintritt kostet.

PAGE 114, EXERCISE S

1. Er **durfte** hier parken.

2. Wir **mussten** uns verkleiden.

3. Du **konntest** ihn kontaktieren.

4. Meine Geschwister **wollten** uns zu Ostern besuchen.

5. Meine Großmutter **sollte** zur Hochzeit kommen.

PAGE 115, EXERCISE T

1. Der Koch **hat** die Forelle **vorbereitet**.

2. Er **hat** meine Kochkenntnisse **diskutiert**.

3. Die Verkäuferin **hat** verschiedene Brotsorten **verkauft**.

4. Du **hast** zu viel Obst **gekauft**.

5. Ihr **habt** die Kalorien **gezählt**.

PAGE 117, EXERCISE U

1. Die Situation **ist** kompliziert geworden.

2. Ein Auto **ist** explodiert.

3. Ich **bin** in die Tschechische Republik gefahren.

4. Nicht viel **ist** in den Ferien passiert.

5. Sie **haben** die Touristen nach Belgien geflogen. (Verb used transitively.)

6. Wann **sind** sie aufgestanden?

7. Wann **sind** Sie in die Stadt gefahren?

8. Was **haben** Sie heute gemacht?

9. Was **hast** du zum Frühstück gegessen?

10. Wie **bist** du hierhergekommen?

PAGE 117, EXERCISE V

(See page 111, Exercise M, **Perfect Tense**, Strong Verbs)

1. Er **hat** sofort zu Aspirin gegriffen.

2. Er **ist** eine Woche im Bett **geblieben**.

3. Die Mutter **hat** eine Geschichte über ein Krankenhaus **geschrieben**.

4. Sie **hat** an Asthma **gelitten**.

5. Sie **hat** sich am Arm **geschnitten**.

6. Der Arzt **ist** in sein Auto **eingestiegen**.

PAGE 117

(See page 112, Exercise N, **Perfect Tense**, Strong Verbs)

1. Sein Koffer **hat** 20 Kilos **gewogen**.

2. Man **hat** die Tür des Flugzeugs **geschlossen**.

3. Er **ist** nach München **geflogen**.

4. Die Stewardess **hat** ein Getränk und einen Imbiss **geboten**.

5. Er **hat** seine Flugtickets **verloren**.

6. Die Touristen **haben gefroren**. (If you said 'sind gefroren' it would mean they were deep frozen.)

PAGE 117

(See page 112, Exercise O, **Perfect Tense**, Strong Verbs)

1. Ich **habe** die Lebkuchen lecker **gefunden**.

2. Er **hat** mich **gezwungen**, zum Weihnachtsmarkt zu gehen.

3. Am Marktplatz hat die Gruppe **begonnen**, Lieder zu singen.

4. Wir **haben** viel Glühwein **getrunken**.

5. Ich **habe** einen Fisch **gewonnen**.

6. Der Fisch **ist** in einem Glas **geschwommen**.

7. Sie **hat** den Sekt **empfohlen**.

8. Ich **habe** ein Glas Pfirsichbowle **genommen**.

9. Wir **haben** uns vor der Konzerthalle **getroffen**.

10. Sie **haben** über die wunderbaren Feuerwerke **gesprochen**.

PAGE 117

(See page 112, Exercise P, **Perfect Tense**, Strong Verbs)

1. Was **ist** in der Imbissstube **geschehen**? (Verbs for 'happening' take *sein*.)

2. Ich **habe** Pizza mit Champignons **gegessen**.

3. Er **hat** mir das Rezept **gegeben**.

4. Er **hat** seinen Termin im Wirtshaus **vergessen**.

5. Sie **hat** im Lokal **gesessen**.

PAGE 117

(See page 112, Exercise Q, **Perfect Tense**, Strong Verbs)

1. Die Gewinne **sind** schnell **gewachsen.**

2. Der Marketing-Manager **ist** nach Frankfurt **gefahren.**

3. Wir **haben** die Konferenz in dem Messezentrum **gehalten.**

4. Ich **habe** meine Dokumente im Büro **gelassen.**

5. Wir **haben** Ihnen **geraten**, die Aktien zu verkaufen.

PAGE 117, EXERCISE W, **PERFECT TENSE**, MIXED VERBS

1. Wir **haben** an die neue Generation **gedacht.**

2. Ich **habe** die Informationen **gesandt.**

3. Er **hat** sich an den Bürgermeister **gewandt.**

4. Er **hat** sie nach Hause **gebracht.** (Note *bringen* where we use 'take' in English.)

5. Ich **habe** die Altstadt sehr gut **gekannt.**

6. Er **hat** alles über die Geschichte der Stadt **gewusst.**

7. Sie **haben** einige interessante Aspekte der Geschichte **genannt.**

8. Ich **habe** an die guten alten Zeiten **gedacht.**

PAGE 118, EXERCISE X

1. Sie **haben** es sehen **wollen.**

2. Ich **habe** es gewollt.

3. Er **hat** den Park besuchen **können.**

4. Sie **hat** ein Tagebuch führen **sollen.** (*ein Tagebuch führen* is the set phrase for writing a diary.)

5. **Haben** Sie die Pauschalreise **gemocht**? (You would be more likely to hear *Hat Ihnen die Pauschalreise gefallen?*)

PAGE 119, EXERCISE Y

1. Der Urlaub **hatte** im Dezember **begonnen.**

2. Herr Boos **war** nach New York **geflogen.**

3. Seine Frau **hatte** einen Billigflug **reserviert.**

4. Er **hatte** seinen Stadtplan **verloren.**

5. Beide **hatten** das Hotel ganz leicht **gefunden.**

6. Zuerst **hatten** sie nicht gut **geschlafen.**

7. Am folgenden Morgen **waren** sie in einen Bus **eingestiegen**.

8. Sie **hatten** die Hauptsehenswürdigkeiten **gesehen**.

9. Jemand **war** von einem Hochhaus **gefallen**.

10. Die Polizei **war** schnell **angekommen**.

PAGE 120, EXERCISE Z

1. Sie **werden** DM2000 **investiert haben**.

2. Er **wird** die Firma in Deutschland **besucht haben**.

3. Sie **werden** einen neuen Marketing-Manager **gefunden haben**.

4. Sie **wird** ein neues Projekt **entwickelt haben**.

5. Ich **werde** das Projekt bis Ende September fertig **haben**. *or* Das Projekt **wird** bis Ende September **fertig**.

PAGE 122, EXERCISE A

1. Unreal.

2. Open.

3. Lost chance.

4. Open.

5. Unreal.

PAGES 122–3, EXERCISE B

1. Ich würde zum Bäcker gehen, wenn sie frische Brötchen verkauften.

2. Sie wird den Mantel kaufen, wenn er billig ist.

3. Sie hätte einen Film gekauft, wenn der Laden auf/geöffnet gewesen wäre.

4. Die Vasen wären billiger gewesen, wenn sie sie in Polen gekauft hätten.

5. Sie werden zum Kaufhaus gehen, wenn sie Zeit haben.

6. Sie würden einen Schirm kaufen, wenn es regnete.

7. Sie hätten uns Karten gegeben, wenn sie gewusst hätten.

8. Wir würden ins Konzert gehen, wenn es möglich wäre.

PAGE 123, EXERCISE C

1. We saw the ducks which were swimming in the water.

2. The children who are looking for eggs are very happy.

3. The biscuits which were baked last week taste super.

4. The nicely packed presents are from my mother.

5. Have you seen the broken window?

PAGE 124, EXERCISE D

1. Während ich Goslar besuchte, sah ich einen Freund/eine Freundin.

2. Wir sahen eine Straßenbahn kommen.

3. Es regnete weiter.

4. Ohne viel zu denken, gingen wir in ein teures Restaurant.

5. Nachdem wir den Führer gekauft hatten, besuchten wir die Burg. (*Wir gingen um die Burg* would mean 'we walked round the outside of the castle'.)

PAGE 124, EXERCISE E

1. Sie sahen meinen Chef, **bevor** er nach Amerika ging.

2. Wir sprachen **vorher** über die Marketing-Probleme.

3. Ich arbeitete **nach** der Wende in Weimar.

4. Sie investierte viel Geld, **nachdem** sie die Firma recherchiert hatte.

5. Er versprach es, **bevor** er viel über die Produkte wusste.

PAGES 125–6, EXERCISE F

1. The birthday cake was baked on Monday.

2. The tickets for the rock concert were sent off yesterday.

3. The presents have been collected the day before yesterday.

4. The Easter eggs were painted by the children.

5. Many eggs were found.

6. The Carnival shop was shut on Sunday.

7. That can be done quickly.

8. There are many costumes to see/to be seen.

9. A lot of people were criticized.

10. That is difficult to explain.

PAGE 126, EXERCISE G

1. Die Karten für das Konzert wurden von meinem Vater reserviert.

2. Die Boutique war geschlossen. (State of events.)

3. Die Verkäuferin hat ihr geholfen. (*helfen* + Dat. so Passive is not possible.)

4. Es gibt viel zu sehen.

5. Viele Menschen wurden im neuen Einkaufszentrum verletzt.

PAGE 127, EXERCISE H

1. Sie wollen schwimmen.

2. Ich hoffe, Tennis zu spielen.

3. Sie sahen ihn Hockey spielen.

4. Sie fuhren nach Wolfsburg, um die Firma zu besuchen.

5. Sie machte es, ohne zum Sportzentrum zu gehen.

PAGE 128, EXERCISE I

1. Darf ich hier parken?

2. Wir können ein Taxi nehmen.

3. Sie kann jeden Moment die Firma besuchen.

4. Sie wollen ins Theater gehen.

5. Sie möchten eine Stadtrundfahrt machen.

6. Sie müssen Karten reservieren.

7. Der Dom muss in der Nähe sein.

8. Wir wollen den Zoo besuchen.

9. Sie sollen zum Fremdenverkehrsamt gehen.

10. Können Sie mir sagen, wo es ist?

PAGE 129, EXERCISE J

1. Ihr ist kalt. (*Sie ist kalt* means 'she is frigid'.)

2. Der Mantel steht ihr gut.

3. Es schneite gestern.

4. Es gelang ihnen.

5. Uns geht es gut.

PAGE 130, EXERCISE K

1. Sie **entschlossen sich,** den Bundestag zu besuchen.

2. Wir **bedankten uns** beim Abgeordneten.

3. Die Mitglieder der Protestgruppe **erkälteten sich**, weil das Wetter so schlecht war.

4. Die norwegische Botschaft **befindet sich** in Berlin.

5. Der Minister **weigerte sich**, mehr zum Thema zu sagen.

PAGE 131, EXERCISE L

1. Sie halfen ihren Kollegen.

2. Er folgte dem Chef.

3. Ihr gefiel das Produkt.

4. Der Computer gehörte mir.

5. Es gelang ihnen, nach Polen zu exportieren.

6. Er widersprach seinem Anwalt.

7. Das neue Gebäude imponierte der Sekretärin.

8. Sie begegneten ihren neuen Kollegen.

9. Sie schmeichelte den Arbeitern.

10. Wir trauten dem Manager.

PAGES 132–3, EXERCISE M

1. Es erinnert mich **an** meine Kindheit.

2. Wir achten **auf** die Zeit.

3. Ich gewöhne mich **an** die Methoden.

4. Er antwortet **auf** die Frage.

5. Es fehlt **an** Musik.

6. Es basiert **auf** Informationen aus dem Internet.

7. Sie ist **an** Lungenkrebs gestorben.

8. Wir warten **auf** die neuen CDs.

9. Sie ging **an** der Kirche vorbei.

10. Ich muss mich **auf** die Hauptprobleme konzentrieren.

PAGE 133, EXERCISE N

1. Es besteht **aus** vielen Teilen (*bestehen* + *auf* = to insist on)

2. Er bedankt sich **für** die Hilfe.

3. Sie müssen **in** die neue Technologie investieren.

4. Sie interessieren sich **für** Computer.

5. Sie haben **mit** Frau Bauer telefoniert.

6. Ich halte das **für** eine gute Idee.

7. Er entschuldigte sich **bei** mir.

8. Sie sorgen **für** die technischen Details.

9. Er hat sich **mit** den neuen Produkten beschäftigt.

10. Sie sorgt **für** die Qualität der Produkte.

PAGE 135, EXERCISE O

1. Viele Teenager halten nicht viel **von** Drogenberatungsstellen.

2. Andere wundern sich **über** die vielen Leute, die Tabletten schlucken.

3. Wenn Leute **von** Drogen abhängen, ist es sehr schwer, weil sie immer Geld brauchen.

4. Einige leiden **an** Essstörungen und werden sehr krank.

5. Lehrer warnen **vor** den Gefahren.

6. Man versucht, Süchtige **zu** einem Rehabilitationsprogramm zu überreden.

7. Viele Jugendliche greifen zu schnell **zu** Drogen.

8. Oft beschweren sie sich **über** den Mangel an Freizeitaktivitäten.

9. Sie sehnen **nach** einem interessanteren Leben.

10. Was verstehen wir **unter** interessant? Schwer zu sagen.

PAGE 138, EXERCISE P

1. Sie sagte, 'Ich habe es getrunken.'

2. Wir sagten, ' Es ist zu spät, ins Restaurant zu gehen.'

3. Sie hatte gesagt, 'Omeletts sind schwer.'

4. Ich habe gesagt, 'Es ist leicht.'

5. Sie sagte, 'Ich werde es versuchen.'

PAGE 138, EXERCISE Q

1. Der Finanzleiter sagte, dass die Firma expandiere.

2. Mein Chef sagte, dass es schwierig wäre.

3. Er sagte, dass er die Lage nicht richtig verstehe.

4. Er sagte, dass sie zu viel in den Nahen Osten investiert hätten.

5. Ich sagte, dass wir leider zu viel verloren hätten.

PAGE 138, EXERCISE R

1. Es wäre schwierig.

2. Es wäre interessanter gewesen.

3. Wenn es geregnet hätte, wäre es eine Katastrophe gewesen.

4. Sie taten so, als wäre es schwierig.

5. Sie hätten das Papier recycelt, wenn sie Zeit gehabt hätten.

11 *Particles, question tags and abbreviations*

PAGES 142–3, EXERCISE A

1. No. Here it means 'Yes'.

2. No. It's a conjunction.

3. Yes.

4. Yes.

5. No. It's an adverb.

6. Yes.

7. No. It's an interjection.

8. No. It's a conjunction.

PAGE 143, EXERCISE B

1. Ich bin **erst** zwei Tage hier.

2. Sie haben **also** nicht viel gesehen?

3. **Doch**, ich habe viele Galerien besucht. (Comes after a negative question.)

4. Aber Sie haben **gar** nicht viel vom Nachtleben gesehen, oder?

5. Erzählen Sie **mal**, was es zu sehen gibt!

6. Ich kann Ihnen **ruhig** einige Clubs empfehlen, aber ich war nie drin.

7. Sie sind **schließlich** viel älter als ich.

8. Leider bin ich **sowieso** zu müde.

9. Das ist **vielleicht** schade!

10. Ich würde **zwar** gerne ausgehen, aber es ist zu spät.

PAGE 144, EXERCISE C

1. My great-aunt's birthday is on Sunday, isn't it?

2. You have got the address already, haven't you?

3. I gave you the invitation, didn't I?

4. People always drink a lot at a party, don't they?

5. We're going to make a peach punch, aren't we?

6. You will bring wine along, won't you?

PAGE 145, EXERCISE D

1. Sie haben *zur Zeit* viele Pauschalreisen im Angebot.

2. *Das heißt*, sie haben natürlich auch Abenteuerreisen, aber sie sind sehr teurer.

3. Sie können *zum Beispiel* eine Safari-Reise machen.

4. Ein Urlaub auf dem Bauernhof *beziehungsweise* auf dem Lande ist für Familien besonders attraktiv.

5. Es gibt *unter anderem* ein Planetarium.

Key to themes

1. Education and business
2. Town and region
3. Environment and weather
4. Media and politics
5. Society and traditions
6. Family and personal
7. Health, sport and drugs
8. Culture and leisure
9. Travel and tourism
10. Food, drink and shopping
11. Miscellaneous

Page	Ex.	1	2	3	4	5	6	7	8	9	10	11
4	A									X		
5	B										X	
6	C			X								
9	D										X	
10	E		X									
11	F											X
12	G								X			
12	H								X			
14	A		X									
16	B									X		
17	C	X										
20	A								X			

Page	Ex.	1	2	3	4	5	6	7	8	9	10	11
21	B								X			
21	C			X								
22	D		X									
23	E								X			
23	F	X										
25	G	X										
26	H								X			
27	I							X				
27	J										X	
28	K										X	
29	L								X			
30	M							X				
30	N									X		
31	O					X						
32	P	X										
33	Q	X										
36	A											X
37	B	X										
38	C	X										
39	D				X							
40	E					X						
41	F											X
42	G										X	
44	H			X								
47	A		X									
48	B											X
49	C		X									
49	D				X							
50	E											X
52	F	X										
54	G				X							
55	H					X						
56	I	X										
58	A						X					

Page	Ex.	1	2	3	4	5	6	7	8	9	10	11
59	B					X						
60	C							X				
61	D			X								
61	E					X						
62	F							X				
64	A										X	
65	B						X					
66	C						X					
67	D	X										
67	E	X										
68	F	X										
69	G						X					
70	H								X			
72	I											X
72	J						X					
74	A									X		
76	B									X		
76	C	X										
78	D			X								
79	E	X										
80	F		X									
81	G										X	
83	H	X										
84	I					X						
85	J						X					
88	A						X					
89	B			X								
90	C									X		
92	D		X									
93	E							X				
94	F									X		
94	G		X									
95	H							X				
98	A	X										

Page	Ex.	1	2	3	4	5	6	7	8	9	10	11
100	B											X
102	C								X			
102	D	X										
103	E	X										
105	F				X							
105	G							X				
106	H									X		
107	I											X
108	J		X									
109	K									X		
110	L								X			
111	M							X				
112	N									X		
112	O					X						
112	P										X	
112	Q	X										
113	R		X									
114	S						X					
115	T										X	
117	U									X		
117	V	X				X		X		X	X	
117	W									X		
118	X									X		
119	Y									X		
120	Z	X										
122	A						X					
122	B										X	
123	C					X						
124	D		X									
124	E	X										
125	F					X						
126	G										X	
127	H							X				
128	I									X		

Page	Ex.	1	2	3	4	5	6	7	8	9	10	11
129	J			X								
130	K				X							
131	L	X										
132	M											X
133	N	X										
135	O							X				
138	P									X		
138	Q	X										
138	R											X
142	A					X						
143	B								X			
144	C					X						
145	D									X		

Irregular verb tables

Infinitive	Meaning	Pres 2 sing if irreg	Pres 3 sing if irreg	Past	Past participle * + sein
backen	to bake	bäckst	bäckt	backte/buk	gebacken
befehlen	to command	befiehlst	befiehlt	befahl	befohlen
beginnen	to begin			begann	begonnen
beißen	to bite	beißt		biss	gebissen
bersten	to burst	birst	birst	barst	*geborsten
betrügen	to deceive			betrog	betrogen
biegen	to bend			bog	gebogen
bieten	to offer	bietest	bietet	bot	geboten
binden	to tie	bindest	bindet	band	gebunden
bitten	to request	bittest	bittet	bat	gebeten
blasen	to blow	bläst	bläst	blies	geblasen
bleiben	to stay			blieb	*geblieben
braten	to roast, fry	brätst	brät	briet	gebraten
brechen	to break	brichst	bricht	brach	gebrochen
brennen	to burn			brannte	gebrannt
bringen	to bring			brachte	gebracht
denken	to think			dachte	gedacht
dringen	to penetrate			drang	*gedrungen
dürfen	to be allowed to	darfst	darf	durfte	dürfen
empfehlen	to recommend	empfiehlst	empfiehlt	empfahl	empfohlen
erschrecken	to be startled	erschrickst	erschrickt	erschrak	*erschrocken

essen	to eat	isst	isst	aß	gegessen
fahren	to drive	fährst	fährt	fuhr	*gefahren
fallen	to fall	fällst	fällt	fiel	*gefallen
fangen	to catch	fängst	fängt	fing	gefangen
finden	to find	findest	findet	fand	gefunden
fliegen	to fly			flog	*geflogen
fliehen	to flee			floh	*geflohen
fließen	to flow	–		floss	*geflossen
fressen	to eat (of animals)	frisst	frisst	fraß	gefressen
frieren	to freeze			fror	gefroren
geben	to give	gibst	gibt	gab	gegeben
gedeihen	to thrive	–		gedieh	*gediehen
gehen	to go			ging	*gegangen
gelingen	to succeed	–		gelang	*gelungen
gelten	to be valid, count as	giltst	gilt	galt	gegolten
genießen	to enjoy	genießt		genoss	genossen
geschehen	to happen	–	geschieht	geschah	*geschehen
gewinnen	to win			gewann	gewonnen
gießen	to pour	gießt		goss	gegossen
gleichen	to resemble			glich	geglichen
gleiten	to slip	gleitest	gleitet	glitt	*geglitten
graben	to dig	gräbst	gräbt	grub	gegraben
greifen	to grasp			griff	gegriffen

Infinitive	Meaning	Pres 2 sing if irreg	Pres 3 sing if irreg	Past	Past participle * + sein
haben	to have	hast	hat	hatte	gehabt
halten	to hold	hältst	hält	hielt	gehalten
hängen	to hang			hing	gehangen
heben	to lift			hob	gehoben
heißen	to be called	heißt		hieß	geheißen
helfen	to help	hilfst	hilft	half	geholfen
kennen	to know			kannte	gekannt
klingen	to sound			klang	geklungen
kommen	to come			kam	*gekommen
können	to be able to	kannst	kann	konnte	**gekonnt/können
kriechen	to creep			kroch	*gekrochen
laden	to load	lädst	lädt	lud	geladen
lassen	to leave/let	lässt	lässt	ließ	gelassen
laufen	to run	läufst	läuft	lief	*gelaufen
leiden	to suffer	leidest	leidet	litt	gelitten
leihen	to lend			lieh	geliehen
lesen	to read	liest	liest	las	gelesen
liegen	to lie			lag	gelegen
lügen	to tell lies			log	gelogen
meiden	to avoid	meidest	meidet	mied	gemieden
messen	to measure	misst	misst	maß	gemessen

misslingen	to fail	—		misslang	*misslungen
mögen	to like	magst	mag	mochte	**gemocht/mögen
müssen	to have to	musst	muss	musste	müssen
nehmen	to take	nimmst	nimmt	nahm	genommen
nennen	to name			nannte	genannt
pfeifen	to whistle			pfiff	gepfiffen
raten	to advise	rätst	rät	riet	geraten
reiben	to rub			rieb	gerieben
reißen	to tear	reißt		riss	gerissen
reiten	to ride	reitest	reitet	ritt	*geritten
rennen	to run			rannte	*gerannt
riechen	to smell			roch	gerochen
ringen	to wrestle			rang	gerungen
rufen	to call			rief	gerufen
saufen	to drink a lot	säufst	säuft	soff	gesoffen
schaffen	to create			schuf	geschaffen
scheiden	to separate	scheidest	scheidet	schied	*geschieden
scheinen	to seem			schien	geschienen
schieben	to push			schob	geschoben
schießen	to shoot	schießt		schoss	geschossen
schlafen	to sleep	schläfst	schläft	schlief	geschlafen
schlagen	to hit	schlägst	schlägt	schlug	geschlagen
schleichen	to creep			schlich	*geschlichen

Infinitive	Meaning	Pres 2 sing if irreg	Pres 3 sing if irreg	Past	Past participle * + sein
schließen	to shut	schließt		schloss	geschlossen
schmeißen	to chuck, throw	schmeißt		schmiss	geschmissen
schmelzen	to melt	–	schmilzt	schmolz	*geschmolzen
schneiden	to cut	schneidest	schneidet	schnitt	geschnitten
schreiben	to write			schrieb	geschrieben
schreien	to shout			schrie	geschrien
schreiten	to step	schreitest	schreitet	schritt	*geschritten
schweigen	to be silent			schwieg	geschwiegen
schwellen	to swell	–	schwillt	schwoll	*geschwollen
schwimmen	to swim			schwamm	*geschwommen
schwingen	to swing			schwang	*geschwungen
schwören	to swear			schwor	geschworen
sehen	to see	siehst	sieht	sah	gesehen
sein	to be	bist	ist	war	*geworden
senden	to send	sendest	sendet	sandte	gesandt
singen	to sing			sang	gesungen
sinken	to sink			sank	*gesunken
sitzen	to sit	sitzt		saß	gesessen
sollen	to be supposed to	sollst	soll	sollte	sollen
sprechen	to speak	sprichst	spricht	sprach	gesprochen
springen	to jump			sprang	*gesprungen

stechen	to stab	stichst	sticht	stach	gestochen
stehen	to stand			stand	gestanden
stehlen	to steal	stiehlst	stiehlt	stahl	gestohlen
steigen	to climb			stieg	*gestiegen
sterben	to die	stirbst	stirbt	starb	*gestorben
stinken	to stink			stank	gestunken
stoßen	to push	stößt	stößt	stieß	gestoßen
streichen	to delete, cut			strich	gestrichen
streiten	to quarrel	streitest	streitet	stritt	gestritten
tragen	to carry	trägst	trägt	trug	getragen
treffen	to meet	triffst	trifft	traf	getroffen
treiben	to drive			trieb	getrieben
treten	to step	trittst	tritt	trat	*getreten
trinken	to drink			trank	getrunken
tun	to do	tust	tut	tat	getan
überwinden	to overcome	überwindest	überwindet	überwand	überwunden
verbergen	to conceal	verbirgst	verbirgt	verbarg	verborgen
verderben	to spoil	verdirbst	verdirbt	verdarb	verdorben
verdrießen	to annoy	verdrießt		verdross	verdrossen
vergessen	to forget	vergisst	vergisst	vergaß	vergessen
verlieren	to lose			verlor	verloren
verschwinden	to disappear	verschwindest	verschwindet	verschwand	*verschwunden
verzeihen	to pardon			verzieh	verziehen

Infinitive	Meaning	Pres 2 sing if irreg	Pres 3 sing if irreg	Past	Past participle * + sein
wachsen	to grow	wächst	wächst	wuchs	*gewachsen
waschen	to wash	wäscht	wäscht	wusch	gewaschen
weben	to weave			wob	gewoben
weichen	to budge			wich	*gewichen
weisen	to point	weist		wies	gewiesen
wenden	to turn	wendest	wendet	wandte	gewandt
werben	to advertise	wirbst	wirbt	warb	geworben
werden	to become	wirst	wird	wurde	*geworden
werfen	to throw	wirfst	wirft	warf	geworfen
wiegen	to weigh			wog	gewogen
winden	to wind	windest	windet	wand	gewunden
wissen	to know	weißt	weiß	wusste	gewusst
wollen	to want to	willst	will	wollte	**gewollt/wollen
ziehen	to pull			zog	gezogen
zwingen	to force			zwang	gezwungen

NB ** See p. 117–18.

Index